Emerging Evidence on Vouchers and Faith-Based Providers in Education

Emerging Evidence on Vouchers and Faith-Based Providers in Education

Case Studies from Africa, Latin America, and Asia

Felipe Barrera-Osorio, Harry Anthony Patrinos, and Quentin Wodon
Editors

THE WORLD BANK
Washington, D.C.

© 2009 The International Bank for Reconstruction and Development / The World Bank

1818 H Street NW
Washington DC 20433
Telephone: 202-473-1000
Internet: www.worldbank.org
E-mail: feedback@worldbank.org

1 2 3 4 12 11 10 09

This volume is a product of the staff of the International Bank for Reconstruction and Development / The World Bank. The findings, interpretations, and conclusions expressed in this volume do not necessarily reflect the views of the Executive Directors of The World Bank or the governments they represent.

The World Bank does not guarantee the accuracy of the data included in this work. The boundaries, colors, denominations, and other information shown on any map in this work do not imply any judgement on the part of The World Bank concerning the legal status of any territory or the endorsement or acceptance of such boundaries.

Rights and Permissions

ISBN: 978-0-8213-7976-9
eISBN: 978-0-8213-7977-6
DOI: 10.1596/978-0-8213-7976-9

Library of Congress Cataloging-in-Publication Data

Emerging evidence on vouchers and faith-based providers / edited by Felipe Barrera-Osorio, Harry Anthony Patrinos, and Quentin Wodon.
    p. cm. — (Directions in development)
  Includes bibliographical references and index.
  ISBN 978-0-8213-7976-9 (alk. paper) — ISBN 978-0-8213-7977-6
  1. Educational vouchers—Developing countries—Case studies. 2. Privatization in education—Developing countries—Case studies. 3. Church schools—Developing countries—Case studies. I. Barrera-Osorio, Felipe. II. Patrinos, Harry Anthony. III. Wodon, Quentin.
  LB2828.7.E47 2009
  379.1'110917242—dc22

                                                                              2009015917

Cover photograph: High school girls taking notes, Suapur, Bangladesh. Scott Wallace / World Bank.
Cover design: Naylor Design.

Contents

Boxes

Figures

Tables

Preface

While public-private partnerships in education in the United States have received a lot of attention, research on such partnerships elsewhere has been very limited—even though they have been steadily gaining prominence, particularly in developing countries. Aiming to fill this gap, this book presents fresh empirical evidence on the effectiveness of various public-private education partnerships from around the world, including voucher programs and faith-based schools. It also compares costs under various systems of service provision.

Part I of *Emerging Evidence on Vouchers and Faith-Based Providers in Education* suggests that voucher schools outperform public schools in the countries studied (Chile and Colombia), but the difference between the various types of schools is not necessarily as large as one might think—and it is certainly smaller than a simple comparison of indicators would suggest—because the ability of parents to choose a school for their child, and of schools to choose the students they admit, diminishes the differences that would have emerged from a random allocation of students.

Part II on faith-based organizations indicates that schools operated by these organizations perform better than public schools in two countries (República Bolivariana de Venezuela and Sierra Leone) but not significantly so in the third country (the Democratic Republic of Congo). In a fourth country (Bangladesh), while public and *madrasa* secondary schools appear to perform equally well, attendance at a *madrasa* at the primary level seems to lower student performance at the secondary level.

Part III on private costs concludes that when school choice is limited, as is the case in the Republic of Korea, parents have been willing to supplement their school's efforts by spending for tutorial or remedial lessons out of pocket. Evidence from Cameroon also suggests that, contrary to popular belief, faith-based schools are not necessarily more targeted toward the poor and are not necessarily cheaper than public schools.

Overall, the case studies in this book provide useful information on the characteristics of students and the performance of various types of schools that benefit from public-private partnerships. While these case studies are empirically grounded, their results are not necessarily of universal application, because context also matters. The authors are careful to point out that while one of the case studies is based on an experiment, the other case studies use instruments or matching methods that have their limitations. Yet a key result from this work is that sound analyses of existing data are feasible and can yield useful conclusions about the contribution that private service providers can offer to educational development. We hope it will encourage more researchers to undertake similar work to demonstrate the many options that developing countries have to reach their education goals.

Elizabeth M. King
Sector Director, Education
Human Development Network
The World Bank

Acknowledgments

This publication is the result of a joint project between the Development Dialogue on Values and Ethics and the Education Group in the Human Development Network at the World Bank. The publication would not have been possible without the contributions of the authors of the country case studies: Hunt Allcott, Prospere Backiny-Yetna, Eric Bettinger, Sebastian Bustos, Dante Contreras, Gregory Elacqua, Tatiana Filgueiras, Charles Goldman, Henk Kok, Changhui Kang, Zahra Kassam, Michael Kremer, Frank Lysy, Karthik Muralidharan, Daniel Ortega, Jon Price, Juan Saavedra, Chris Sakellariou, Felipe Salazar, Paulina Sepulveda, Clarence Tsimpo, and Yvonne Ying.

Some papers were presented at a World Bank international seminar on the empirical evidence of Public-Private Partnerships (PPPs) in Education. The aim of the seminar was to examine the impact of PPPs on educational outcomes around the world, with an emphasis on developing countries and on papers with solid, credible identification strategies. The Organizing Committee for this seminar consisted of Harry Anthony Patrinos, Paul Peterson of Harvard University, Elizabeth King, and Felipe Barrera-Osorio. We would like to thank the seminar chairs and discussants: Cristian Aedo, Erik Bloom, Amit Dar, Guy Ellena, Robin Horn, Emmanuel Jimenez, Ruth Kagia, Maureen Lewis, Sebastian Martinez, Juan Carlos Navarro, Halsey

Rogers, Tanya Scobie, Emmanuel Skoufias, and Emiliana Vegas—and especially Paul Peterson and Elizabeth King.

The organizational and logistical support received from Shaista Baksh is gratefully acknowledged. Editorial work was provided by Fiona Mcintosh and Juan Carlos Parra Osorio. Veronica Grigera's contribution in bringing the book together is gratefully acknowledged, as is the support of the production team of the Office of the Publisher, including Aziz Gokdemir, Paola Scalabrin, and Denise Bergeron. Finally, we would like to thank our management, especially Joy Phumaphi, Elizabeth King, Rakesh Nangia, and Robin Horn, for encouraging us in putting the book together.

About the Authors

Hunt Allcott is a PhD student in Public Policy, Harvard University.

Mohammad Niaz Asadullah is a Consultant at the South Asia Human Development Sector, the World Bank.

Prospere Backiny-Yetna is a Consultant with the Development Dialogue on Values and Ethics unit at the World Bank.

Eric Bettinger is at the Stanford School of Education, Stanford University.

Sebastian Bustos is at the Department of Economics, Universidad de Chile.

Nazmul Chaudhury is a Senior Economist at the South Asia Human Development Sector, the World Bank.

Dante Contreras is at the Centro de Microdatos (Iniciativa Milenio), Universidad de Chile.

Amit Dar is Sector Manager, Education, for the South Asia Human Development Sector, the World Bank.

Gregory Elacqua is at the Centro de Políticas Comparadas de Educación (Center for Comparative Education Policy), Universidad Diego Portales, Chile.

Changhui Kang is an Associate Professor, Department of Economics, Chung-Ang University, the Republic of Korea.

Michael Kremer is the Gates Professor of Developing Societies in the Department of Economics at Harvard University and Senior Fellow at the Brookings Institution.

Daniel E. Ortega is at the Corporación Andina de Fomento (CAF) and the Instituto de Estudios Superiores de Administracion (IESA), Caracas, República Bolivariana de Venezuela.

Juan E. Saavedra is a PhD candidate in Public Policy, Harvard University.

Chris Sakellariou is an Associate Professor at the School of Humanities, Arts and Social Sciences, Nanyang Technological University in Singapore.

Felipe Salazar is a Researcher at the Center for Comparative Education Policy, Universidad Diego Portales, Chile.

Paulina Sepulveda is at the Department of Economics, Universidad de Chile.

Clarence Tsimpo is a Consultant with the Development Dialogue on Values and Ethics unit at the World Bank.

Yvonne Ying is a Consultant with the Development Dialogue on Values and Ethics at the World Bank.

About the Editors

Felipe Barrera-Osorio is a Senior Education Economist at the Human Development Network, Education Sector, the World Bank.

Harry Anthony Patrinos is a Lead Education Economist at the Human Development Network, Education Sector, the World Bank.

Quentin Wodon is the Adviser and Program Manager for the Development Dialogue on Values and Ethics unit, the Human Development Network, the World Bank.

Abbreviations

AIR	American Institutes for Research
ATE	average treatment effect
CSAT	College Scholastic Ability Test (Republic of Korea)
EMO	education management organization
FBO	faith-based organization
FSP	Female Stipend Program (Bangladesh)
FSSAP	Female Secondary School Assistance Program
IALS	International Adult Literary Survey
ICFES	Colombia's centralized college entrance examination
IEA	International Association for the Evaluation of Education Advancement
IV	instrumental variable
KEDI	Korea Educational Development Institute
KEEP	Korea Education and Employment Panel
KRIVET	Korea Research Institute for Vocational Education and Training
MEST	Ministry of Education, Sports, and Technology (Sierra Leone)
NELS	National Educational Longitudinal Studies
NGO	nongovernmental organization
OECD	Organisation for Economic Co-operation and Development

OLS	ordinary least squares
PAA	Prueba de Aptitud Académica (Venezuelan equivalent of the SAT)
PACES	Programa de Aplicación de Cobertura de la Educación Secundaria
PPs	private fee-paying establishments (Chile)
PPP	public-private partnership
PSs	subsidized establishments (Chile)
PSU	Primary Sampling Unit
PUs	municipal establishments (Chile)
SIMCE	System of Measurement of the Quality of Education
SLIHS	Sierra Leone Integrated Household Survey
SRI	Stanford Research Institute
SSC	high school examination (Bangladesh)
TIMSS	Trends in International Mathematics and Science Study

CHAPTER 1

Public-Private Partnerships in Education: An Overview

Felipe Barrera-Osorio, Harry Anthony Patrinos, and Quentin Wodon

Introduction

Although governments remain the primary financiers of education worldwide (at least for compulsory basic education), in many countries a substantial share of education facilities are operated by private entities. Private schools, and more generally public-private partnerships (PPPs), are often said to increase parents' and students' choices in the types of services available to them. This increase in choice may lead to competition in the school system, potentially leading to efficiency gains and improved quality (Hoxby 1994). Private schools may also make schooling available in places in which public schools are simply not present or in which they lack the capacity to serve all children. This is often the case with nonprofit and faith-based schools located in very poor neighborhoods or in areas of countries affected by conflict in which the state has failed to provide services. Private schools can also provide services considered important by parents that are not provided in public schools. In the case of faith-based schools, these services may entail an emphasis on religious education apart from the standard curriculum or simply an emphasis on ethical values. In the case of private for-profit schools, selection at entry and higher fees paid by parents may enable the schools to provide a higher-quality education to the fortunate students who are able to attend.

The role of private schools appears to be especially important in a context in which, despite the clear commitment of governments and international agencies to the education sector, efficient and equitable access to education still proves elusive to many. This is readily visible in simple statistics of enrollment rates according to the poverty status of children—in most countries, and especially in the poorest countries, enrollment rates are much lower in the lower quintiles of the distribution of income or consumption than in the upper quintiles. Access issues are being addressed with a range of international initiatives, including the Fast Track Initiative (FTI 2005) whereby resources are being channeled to low-income countries to help them achieve universal basic education, a key target under the Millennium Development Goals. However, even in cases in which children do have access to education facilities, the quality of education is often poor (Hanushek and Woessmann 2007). This had been increasingly apparent in the international learning test scores, in which most students from developing countries fail to excel (Woessmann 2005).

Private education and PPPs are no panacea for solving these problems, but they can help in making progress. PPPs encompass a wide range of providers, including for-profit schools (that operate as enterprises), religious schools, nonprofit schools run by nongovernmental organizations (NGOs), publicly funded schools operated by private boards, and community-owned schools. By extending support to nonpublic schools and providing financing, either through school grants or vouchers, governments can provide better choices for parents and an opportunity to fully participate in their children's schooling. Yet the empirical evidence on the efficiency of such approaches is still limited, and considerable controversy exists. While there is surging demand for private education in response to limited public access and poor quality in many countries, there is a need to ensure equity and efficiency in targeted interventions funded through PPPs, and this in turn requires rigorous impact evaluation.

The provision of publicly funded private education raises a number of difficult ethical and strategic issues. We will not discuss those issues in this book, however. Instead, our objective is more focused. This book aims to provide a set of empirical case studies on the performance of different types of schools within the context of PPPs, with a focus for the most part on education outcomes such as test scores and basic literacy and numeracy, but also with attention on some ways in which PPPs are functioning, including the cost of private schools for students.

All the chapters in this book are based on rigorous analysis of survey data, with due attention paid to the issue of endogeneity in the choice of schools by parents. The issue of endogeneity relates to the fact that the school choice parents make is not independent of the performance of the children. For example, if parents are willing to pay more for the education of their brightest children in private schools because they believe that these children will benefit from a better education in these schools, the test scores of the students in private schools may be higher than in public schools simply because they attract brighter children, and not necessarily because the private schools provide a better, or value-added, education. The same issue of endogeneity occurs when the schools are making the selection, instead of the parents. Endogeneity of school choice is an issue when attempting to compare the cost of different schools or when assessing the impact that expenditures on private tutoring have on test scores. The distinctive characteristic of all the chapters in this book is that they all aim to assess performance in a rigorous way by using appropriate econometric techniques in the analysis to weed out the issue of endogeneity.

About half the chapters included in the book are derived from studies presented at an international conference organized at the World Bank in 2007 on the empirical evidence concerning the performance of PPPs in education. The objective of the conference was to examine the impact of PPPs on education outcomes, with an emphasis on less developed and developing countries. The papers selected for the conference were those deemed to have solid, credible identification strategies to deal with the endogeneity issue mentioned above. Because most of the papers presented at the conference dealt with voucher-based schools in Latin America, a number of additional studies were later prepared to expand the geographic scope (to consider case studies from sub-Saharan Africa and Asia) and the thematic scope of the book (to deal with service provision by faith-based schools and the private cost of schooling).

Definition, Typology, and Potential Advantages of Public-Private Partnerships

The definition of a public-private partnership is not clear-cut. To some it is a risk-sharing relationship, whereas for others it is more of a cooperative venture between the public and private sectors. Clearly, the definitions differ in regard to scope and formality of arrangements. A more comprehensive definition is that a PPP is a contracting mechanism used to acquire a specified service, of a defined quantity and quality, at an agreed-on price, from a specific provider, for a specific period (Taylor 2003). Both the capacity to honor contracts and the technical capability of the public sector to structure and monitor these contracts are critical, especially for more complex and long-term contracts. In short, the definition of a public-private partnership implies a strong contracting system on the part of the state.

This definition encompasses three key aspects of the alliance between the public and private sectors. First, a PPP contract can achieve an optimal level of risk sharing between the government and the private sector. The change to an optimal level of risk sharing may increase efficiency in the delivery of services, and as a consequence, it may induce more resources and provision of education. Second, the contract recognizes the complementary role of the public and private sectors. Finally, another characteristic of the PPP, according to this definition, is that the agreement is outcome focused; for example, it clearly stipulates aspects such as the quality and the quantity of the expected outcome.

Several types of contracts, depending on the specific services that are provided, can be analyzed using this definition. The contracts observed in practice indeed vary in their degree of complexity. For the case of education, the services can be construction of infrastructure; management, maintenance, and services contracts; or education services and education operations (see LaRocque and Patrinos 2006; World Bank 2006).

Education operations contracts are, in general, complex contracts. Delivery of education can be measured through the number of children enrolled, but school attendance does not mean that students are learning. Observing final outputs such as test scores is often difficult and requires specific data collection efforts. Moreover, learning depends heavily on family background, a factor that the school cannot control. In short, PPP contracts are difficult to establish and usually require long-term commitments. The studies of faith-based schools in this book for Bangladesh, the Democratic Republic of Congo, Sierra Leone, and República Bolivariana de Venezuela are examples of education operations, but the formality of the contracts used in the different countries vary greatly. Vouchers and services (food, maintaining infrastructure) may be less complicated contracts. Quantification of the actual good is easier; the time frame may be shorter. Each of these contracts may work differently, depending on the technical capacity and the degree of development of each country's rule of law, because countries differ in these aspects. Probably less complex contracts can work more efficiently in low-income countries; more complex contracts require more legal and technical development (see table 1.1).

Table 1.1 Types of Contracts in Education

Objective of contract	Definition	Contract types
Management, professional services (input)	Government buys school management services or auxiliary and professional services.	Management contracts Professional services contract (curriculum design)
Operation services (process)	Government buys school operation services.	Operational contracts
Education services (output)	Government buys student places in private schools (contracts with school to enroll specific students).	Contract for education of specific students
Facility availability (input)	Government buys facility availability.	Provision of infrastructure services contracts
Facility availability and education services (input and output bundle)	Government buys facility availability combined with services (operational or outputs).	Provision of infrastructure contracts with education services contracts

Source: World Bank 2006.

Four main arguments have been used in the literature to suggest a positive relationship between PPPs and the quality of education as well as gains in enrollment (see Epple and Romano 1998; LaRocque and Patrinos 2006; Nechyba 2000; Savas 2000):

1. PPPs can induce competition in the market for education. The private sector can compete with the public sector for students. In turn, the public sector may react to the competition via increments in the quality of education.
2. A PPP contract may be more flexible than most contracts in the public sector. Generally, the public sector has a high degree of inflexibility in hiring teachers and organizing schools. By contrast, PPPs offer flexibility in those areas. The flexibility of the contract can create a better fit between the supply and demand of education.
3. At least in middle-income countries, private providers in PPP contracts usually are chosen by open bid following quality criteria. Contracts usually contain clauses stipulating the delivery of a certain quality of education, and the best proposals are chosen. By itself, this characteristic of the contract can increase the quality of education.
4. A PPP contract can achieve an optimal level of risk sharing between the government and the private sector. The change to an optimal level of risk sharing may increase efficiency in the delivery of services, and consequently, it may induce the provision of more resources in the education sector.

Much of the literature on PPPs has focused on high- and middle-income countries, in which the arguments described above are the main arguments used to defend PPPs. Yet, PPPs also exist in low-income countries (see Chakrabarti and Peterson 2008; Patrinos et all. 2009) in which the market share of private education providers is actually often significantly higher than in middle- and high-income countries. In postconflict countries in sub-Saharan Africa, for example, where the state has not been able to expand services because of weak budgets and capacity, it is not uncommon for private providers to provide half or even in some cases a higher share of the education services used by children and youth. In other low-income countries, the market share of private institutions is lower, but still significant, as a result of either history (the role of missionary schools before independence) or poor performance (the rise of private schools for the more affluent population in urban areas).

Issues of competition, open bids with selection based on quality, and optimality of risk sharing are often not at the core of the debate

Figure 1.1   Provisions and Financing of Education Options

		Provision	
		Private	**Public**
Finance	**Private**	• Private schools • Private universities • Home schooling • Tutoring	• User fees • Student loans
	Public	• Vouchers • Contract schools • Charter schools • Contracting out	• Public schools • Public universities

Source: Patrinos et al. 2009.

in low-income countries, but the issue of flexibility is important because public school teachers often benefit from substantial advantages and the demographic pressure forces governments to try to reduce teacher costs in a context in which tax revenues are severely limited. Still, in most low-income countries, beyond flexibility the key issue remains to make basic education available to more children. Rural and low-income families, girls, indigenous peoples, and other poor and marginalized groups still lack access to education; and the quality of education, as measured for example by standardized tests, is also a major challenge.

To sum up, in both low- and middle-income countries, the collaboration of the public and private sectors can help to overcome the specific (and often different) challenges faced in various countries. In a context of market failures and positive externalities, as well as capital market imperfections and equity concerns, governments have an important space for intervention in education through the public sector, but they should also consider the full variety of policy instruments at their disposal to meet education objectives (figure 1.1 lists some of those instruments as to whether the financing and provision are public or private). In short, PPPs recognize that governments can meet their policy objectives using different service delivery models—not just the "traditional" publicly financed and delivered service.

Contributions in This Book

Although PPPs in education in the United States have received a great deal of attention, research on such partnerships in other parts of the world has been very limited. However, PPPs play an important role in the provision of education outside the United States, and their importance has been steadily rising, particularly in developing countries. The chapters in this book present new and fresh empirical evidence on the effectiveness of various PPPs from different parts of the world.

Chapters 2 through 5 (part 1 of this book) are devoted to empirical work on voucher schools. Of the four chapters, three are motivated by Chile's experience. Since 1981, students and their families have been given school choice, with equal funding of public and private schools. Chile's voucher experience has generated a great deal of interest, with a number of studies, but the experience remains controversial. Although some researchers claim that vouchers lead to improved outcomes, others come to the opposite conclusion. There is a strong element of selection in Chile's voucher program and evidence that the program has led to sorting.

In chapter 2, Elacqua, Contreras, and Salazar (2009) take up the debate about the size of school operations. They use 2002 data on more than 220,000 fourth graders to compare Spanish and mathematics achievement in private school franchises, private independent schools, and public schools. Their findings suggest that franchises have a large advantage over public schools, once student and peer attributes and selectivity are controlled for. It appears however that there is no statistically significant difference in achievement between public and private independent voucher schools. They also find that further disaggregating private voucher school franchises reduces the small franchise advantages and widens the larger franchise advantages.

In chapter 3, Patrinos and Sakellariou (2009) use unique information on cognitive ability contained in the International Adult Literacy Survey (IALS) and the 1981 vouchers reform in Chile to create a binary instrument to control for endogeneity in school choice. They find that the main beneficiaries of the reform were those who at the time were entering primary school or who were existing pupils in basic education. For this treated group of pupils, only a small part of the estimated return to schooling is due to classic ability bias. However, once the treated group is expanded to include secondary school students, the pure return to schooling decreases dramatically, whereas the return to cognitive skills is very large, suggesting that most of the estimated return from a Mincerian earnings function is due to classic ability bias.

In chapter 4, Contreras, Bustos, and Sepulveda (2009) argue that the Chilean voucher scheme allows for-profit private subsidized schools to choose their students. Their study examines the effects of this practice on the results gap between private and public schools and its impact on academic performance. They present evidence indicating that student selection is a widespread practice among private subsidized schools. The evidence, after controlling for a series of selection criteria and the segmentation effects that they produce, suggests that there are no differences in results between public and private subsidized education. Yet a student attending a school that uses selection criteria obtains results in standardized mathematics tests that are, on average, between 6 percent and 14 percent higher than those obtained by a student from a school that does not use selection.

Chapter 5 relies on a randomized experiment. Bettinger, Kremer, and Saavedra (2009) challenge the view that vouchers benefit recipients only by improving their peer groups at the expense of others. Their paper takes advantage of an education voucher program in Colombia, for which spots were allocated by lottery, to identify a set of applicants for whom winning the voucher did not lead to attending schools with peers with superior observable characteristics. In particular, they focus on students who applied to vocational private schools. In this population, lottery losers rather than winners were more likely to attend academic secondary schools. Despite this, they find that even in this population, lottery winners had better education outcomes, including higher graduation rates and reading test scores. This casts doubt on the argument that voucher effects operate entirely through improving the set of peers available to recipients. One hypothesis is that private vocational schools are better than public schools at adjusting to the demands of the labor market. Consistent with this hypothesis, private vocational schools are overwhelmingly concentrated on teaching skills that prepare students for Colombia's rapidly growing service sector, whereas public vocational schools are more likely to teach industrial curricula that prepare students for more traditional blue-collar positions.

Chapters 6 through 9 (part 2) are devoted to the provision of education services by faith-based organizations (FBOs). In chapter 6, Allcott and Ortega (2009) look at the performance of Fe y Alegría schools in R. B. de Venezuela. Fe y Alegría is a confederation of Jesuit schools targeting disadvantaged youth. The organization serves more than 1.2 million students in 15 Latin American countries. Most observers consider Fe y Alegría to be successful, but few rigorous evaluations have been undertaken until now. Allcott and Ortega use propensity score matching methods to estimate the effects on standardized test scores of students from the Fe y Alegría private school system in R. B. de Venezuela and compare these schools with public schools. They find an average treatment effect on the order of 0.1 standard deviation in mathematics, which is small, but nevertheless statistically significant. They argue that the better performance of the Fe y Alegría system stems not only from its labor contract flexibility and decentralized administrative structure, but also from the peculiar "family culture" of the schools.

Chapters 7 and 8 are devoted to a comparison of faith-based and public schools in Sierra Leone (Quentin Wodon and Yvonne Ying 2009) and the Democratic Republic of Congo (Backiny-Yetna and Wodon 2009). As a result of both history (the legacy of missionary schools that were established before independence) and the fact that conflict has prevented the state from establishing well-functioning national school systems, faith-based schools account for a majority of students in both countries. However, in both countries the schools benefit from funding from the state. Faith-based schools appear to be serving especially poor children in Sierra Leone; and in the Democratic Republic of Congo, they simply serve most of the children, a large majority of whom are poor. The data used for the two chapters are from nationally representative integrated surveys, so that no test scores are available. However, information is available on parents' subjective perceptions concerning the literacy and numeracy of their children, as well as on other indicators of performance, such as dropout and grade repetition. Although basic statistics suggest that in Sierra Leone children in faith-based schools perform slightly less well than children in public schools, those numbers do not account for the fact that faith-based schools serve poorer children, nor do they control for endogeneity in school choice. With proper controls (using the community market shares of various types of schools as a determinant of individual school choice, but not of performance conditional on school choice), faith-based schools are shown to actually perform better than public schools, and the differences are not negligible. In contrast, in the Democratic Republic of Congo, there are few statistically significant differences in performance between faith-based and public schools after controlling for the types of students attending the schools and the endogeneity of school choice.

In chapter 9, Asadullah, Chaudhury, and Dar (2009) look at the impact of school characteristics on secondary student achievement using a rich data set from rural Bangladesh. By using a combination of fixed effects and instrumental variable estimation techniques, they deal with the selectivity issue coming from the nonrandom sorting of children into religious schools. In addition, they use the class-size variation between two classrooms of the same grade within individual schools to identify causal class-size effects. Their empirical results do not reveal any difference in test scores between religious (madrasas) and secular schools when selection into religious school is taken into account. Yet they do document a statistically significant learning deficit for graduates of primary madrasas who tend to have lower test scores in secondary schools even after controlling for school- and classroom-specific unobservable correlates of learning.

The last chapters (part 3) are devoted to the private cost of schooling under various systems of service provision. The causal relationship between education spending and student outcomes has attracted substantial attention in the literature, but most studies have examined the effectiveness of public school expenditures on student outcomes. In chapter 10, Kang (2009) sheds light on the impacts of education inputs by examining a private education investment, that of private tutoring in South Korea. The context in Korea is one in which school choice is rather limited, so that many parents invest in the education of their children in a different way to improve schooling outcomes. To deal with the endogeneity of private tutoring expenditures, Kang relies on instrumental variables methods by exploiting a student's birth order as a source of identification. His results suggest that a 10 percent increase in expenditure leads to a 0.56 percentile point improvement in test scores. This effect is modest but comparable to the effect of public school expenditures on earnings estimated by previous studies.

In chapter 11, Backiny-Yetna and Wodon (2009b) compare the fees paid to public and faith-based schools in Cameroon. It is often argued that faith-based schools tend to be better targeted to the poor than is the case for the public sector (and certainly for the private for-profit sector). Yet this may depend on the type of PPP in place in any given country. In Cameroon, faith-based schools serve better-off children compared to public schools, probably in large part because they are more expensive. This, in turn, is related to the fact that public subsidies provided per student to faith-based schools are smaller than those for public schools. To assess how much more expensive faith-based schools are, econometrics again have to be used. Because faith-based schools are more expensive than public schools, parents who can afford these schools are likely to be able and willing to spend more on the education of their children, and that may generate an upward bias in the comparison of the cost of schooling between faith-based and public schools. The results of the econometric estimates suggest that for similar students, faith-based schools cost about 40 percent more than public schools in Cameroon.

Conclusion

The first part of the book, devoted to vouchers, suggests that voucher schools outperform public schools in both Chile and Colombia. In the case of Chile the difference between the various types of schools is not necessarily large, and it is certainly smaller than simple statistics would suggest as a result of school selection by both parents and the schools.

The second set of chapters suggests that faith-based schools perform better than public schools in two countries (R. B. de Venezuela and Sierra Leone), but that there are few statistically significant differences in the third country (the Democratic Republic of Congo). In the last country (Bangladesh), whereas public and madrasa secondary schools perform equally well, having gone to a primary madrasa may have a negative effect on student performance in secondary schools.

The chapters in the third part of the book suggest that when school choice is limited, as is the case in Korea, parents can still influence the performance of their children through private expenditure for tutoring. The papers also suggest that, contrary to popular belief, faith-based schools are not necessarily more targeted toward the poor. In Cameroon, probably in large part because faith-based schools do not receive the same level of funding as public schools, they are more expensive for parents, and for that reason they tend to serve a population that is wealthier than the population using the public schools. At the same time, perhaps because of higher private funding, corruption in faith-based schools tends to be lower than in public schools, which may then improve the satisfaction of parents with faith-based schools as compared with public schools. In this regard, the role of the government as a regulator is critical. Moreover, the contract for the provision of education between the government and the private sector can include clauses toward correction of inequalities of opportunity.

From a technical point of view, it is worth recalling that the identification strategies used in the various chapters in this book are not without limits. Although the results obtained appear to be reasonable, only one of the case studies relies on an experiment. All the other case studies rely on instruments or matching methods that are known to be imperfect. Thus, the case studies suggest that it is feasible to conduct empirical work on the performance of publicly funded private schools with typical cross-sectional data. However, it is important not to oversell the results presented here, which would benefit from further validation using other data.

To conclude, the case studies in this book provide useful information on the characteristics of the student body and on the performance of various types of schools that benefit from public-private partnerships, but they do not necessarily provide results that are of universal application, because the empirical evidence that emerges from the analysis tends to be country-specific. This also suggests that to consider policy options for public-private partnerships in any given country, it is essential to conduct detailed empirical work on the data for that country. We hope that the case studies presented in this book will inspire many others.

References

Allcott, H., and D. E. Ortega. 2009. "The Performance of Decentralized School Systems: Evidence from Fe y Alegría in Venezuela." In *Emerging Evidence on Private Participation in Education: Vouchers and Faith-Based Providers*, ed. F. Barrera-Osorio, H. A. Patrinos, and Q. Wodon. Washington, DC: World Bank.

Asadullah, M. N., N. Chaudhury, and A. Dar. 2009. "Student Achievement in Religious and Secular Secondary Schools in Bangladesh." In *Emerging Evidence on Private Participation in Education: Vouchers and Faith-Based Providers*, F. Barrera-Osorio, H. A. Patrinos, and Q. Wodon. Washington, DC: World Bank.

Backiny-Yetna, P. and Q. Wodon. 2009a. "Comparing Faith-Based and Government Schools in the Democratic Republic of Congo." In *Emerging Evidence on Private Participation in Education: Vouchers and Faith-Based Providers*, ed. F. Barrera-Osorio, H. A. Patrinos, and Q. Wodon. Washington, DC: World Bank.

Backiny-Yetna, P., and Q. Wodon. 2009b. "Comparing the Cost of Public, Religious, and Private Schooling in Cameroon." In *Emerging Evidence on Private Participation in Education: Vouchers and Faith-Based Providers*, ed. F. Barrera-Osorio, H. A. Patrinos, and Q. Wodon. Washington, DC: World Bank.

Bettinger, E., M. Kremer, and J. E. Saavedra. 2009. "How Do Vouchers Work? Evidence from Colombia." In *Emerging Evidence on Private Participation in Education: Vouchers and Faith-Based Providers*, ed. F. Barrera-Osorio, H. A. Patrinos, and Q. Wodon. Washington, DC: World Bank.

Chakrabarti, F. and P. Peterson. 2009. *School Choice International.* Cambridge, MA: MIT Press.

Contreras, D., S. Bustos, and P. Sepulveda. 2009. "When Schools Are the Ones That Choose: The Effect of Screening in Chile." In *Emerging Evidence on Private Participation in Education: Vouchers and Faith-Based Providers,* ed. F. Barrera-Osorio, H. A. Patrinos, and Q. Wodon. Washington, DC: World Bank.

Elacqua, G., D. Contreras, and F. Salazar. 2009. "The Effectiveness of Franchises and Independent Private Schools in Chile's National Voucher Program." In *Emerging Evidence on Private Participation in Education: Vouchers and Faith-Based Providers,* ed. Felipe F. Barrera-Osorio, H. A. Patrinos, and Q. Wodon. Washington, DC: World Bank.

Epple, D., and R. E. Romano. 1998. "Competition between Private and Public Schools, Vouchers, and Peer-Group Effects." *American Economic Review* 88 (1): 33–62.

FTI Secretariat. 2005. *Fast Track Initiative: Building a Global Compact for Education.* Washington, DC: World Bank, Education Notes series.

Hoxby, C. M. 1994. "Do Private Schools Provide Competition for Public Schools?" NBER (National Bureau of Economic Research) Working Paper 4978. NBER, Cambridge, MA.

Hanushek, E. A., and L. Woessmann. 2007. *Education Quality and Economic Growth.* Washington, DC: World Bank.

Kang, C. 2009. "Does Money Matter? The Effect of Private Education Expenditures on Academic Performance." In *Emerging Evidence on Private Participation in Education: Vouchers and Faith-Based Providers,* ed. F. Barrera-Osorio, H. A. Patrinos, and Q. Wodon. Washington, DC: World Bank.

LaRocque, N., and H. Patrinos. 2006. "Choice and Contracting Mechanisms in the Education Sector." World Bank, Washington, DC.

Nechyba, T. J. 2000. "Mobility, Targeting and Private School Vouchers." *American Economic Review* 90 (1): 130–46.

Patrinos, H. A., F. Barrera-Osorio, and J. Guaqueta. 2009. *The Role and Impact of Public-Private Partnerships in Education.* Washington, DC: World Bank.

Patrinos, H. A., and C. Sakellariou. 2009. "Cognitive Ability, Heterogeneity, Endogeneity, and Returns to Schooling in Chile: Outcomes of the 1981 Capitation Grant Scheme." In *Emerging Evidence on Private Participation in Education: Vouchers and Faith-Based Providers,* ed. F. Barrera-Osorio, H. A. Patrinos, and Q. Wodon. Washington, DC: World Bank.

Savas, E. S 2000. *Privatization and Public-Private Partnerships.* New York: Chatham House Publishers.

Taylor, R. J. 2003. "Contracting for Health Services." In *Private Participation in Health Services Handbook*, ed. A. Harding and A. Preker. Washington, DC: World Bank.

Wodon, Q., and Y. Ying. 2009."Literacy and Numeracy in Faith-Based and Government Schools in Sierra Leone." In *Emerging Evidence on Private Participation in Education: Vouchers and Faith-Based Providers*, ed. F. Barrera-Osorio, H. A. Patrinos, and Q. Wodon. Washington, DC: World Bank.

World Bank. 2006. "Colombia Contracting Education Services." Report 31841-CO. World Bank, Washington, DC.

PART I

Vouchers

CHAPTER 2

The Effectiveness of Franchises and Independent Private Schools in Chile's National Voucher Program

Gregory Elacqua, Dante Contreras, and Felipe Salazar

Introduction

The optimal scale of school operations is one of the most hotly debated issues in current education policy reform discussions. One view is that larger schooling operations offer education services more effectively than small independent schools. Proponents argue that increasing the size of schooling operations would lower per-pupil costs and free resources for use at the school and classroom level (Chubb 2001). Advocates also argue that with larger schooling operations there will be more opportunities to access private investments and loans to expand than with smaller operations (Whittle 2000).

Researchers also claim that private school franchises promote the creation of sound institutional environments in member schools. McMeekin

For generous feedback, we would like to thank Cristian Aedo, Herald Beyer, Francisco Gallego, Harry Patrinos, Paul Peterson, and Daniel Ortega. This chapter also benefited from discussions with John Londregan, Martin Gilens, Henry Levin, Mark Schneider, Jack Buckley, Elif Calki, Andrew Owen, and David Glick. We thank the Chilean Ministry of Education for providing the data. Any remaining errors are the authors'.

(2003) argues that being part of a franchise provides a sharing experience within the network and facilitates the flow of information (such as research on best practices) to network members. Proponents also maintain that school franchises provide political benefits and credibility and legitimacy in the eyes of the community. Wohlstetter and her colleagues (2004) maintain, based on their research of charter school partnerships in the United States, that well-established charter school networks can build credibility for fundraising more easily than small independent charter schools. The basic hypothesis of these theories is that, all else being equal, the more a schooling organization facilitates transactions between members of a school's community, the better the school's performance.

These assertions have sparked two different trends in school management: consolidating public school districts and increasing public funding for private and charter school franchises and education management organizations (EMOs). Both gained legitimacy from research suggesting that there were inefficiencies present in the traditional public school systems (Hoxby 1994) and from the belief that there are economies of scale in education (Chubb 2001). Underlying the public school district consolidation movement is a belief that consolidation is a way for school districts to cut costs (Duncombe and Yinger 2005) and to improve how education services are delivered (Smith and Wohlstetter 2001). Underlying the privatization movement is the belief that by introducing competition and a business approach to schooling, schools will succeed (or fail) as firms do (Whittle 2000) and that private and charter school franchises and schools run by EMOs will produce education outcomes more effectively and efficiently than public schools and small independent schools (Chubb 2001).

Critics fear that these reforms could potentially have negative unintended consequences. They argue that large centralized operations will create hard-to-manage bureaucracies and foster diseconomies of scale as a result of associated problems of managing complex organizations, maintaining order, and creating a sense of community among students, parents, teachers, and administrators (Brown et al. 2004; Steifel et al. 2000). Opponents of school consolidation also claim that large schooling operations would empower administrators and other professionals far removed from the classroom (Hill et al. 1997). Others are concerned that consolidation reforms would encourage more standardization and less innovation. For instance, Belfield and Levin (2005) maintain that school franchises must establish a brand to be successful, which necessitates relatively uniform operations and services from site to site. They argue that such a branded approach to education would stifle innovation.

Some have argued that reducing the size of schooling operations is a more effective way to improve education outcomes. They claim that small autonomous schools can improve the quality of education by creating intimate learning communities in which students are encouraged by educators who know them (Wasley et al. 2000). Small school advocates also argue that small schools reduce the anonymity and isolation that many students experience in larger schooling operations and that they increase students' sense of belonging (Barker and Gump 1964). Proponents also argue that smaller schools have higher levels of cooperation between teachers, better relations with school administrators, and higher trust in the school community (Lee and Loeb 2000). In addition, they maintain that small schools will encourage parental involvement, which benefits students and the entire community (see, for example, Schneider et al. 2000).

Following these insights, many current proposals for reform in the United States share a vision of small, autonomous schools, with a lean administrative structure, encouraged to bring parents, students, teachers, and administrators into supportive relationships (Raywid 1998). In this vision of small schools, teachers and parents are viewed as essential to school governance and to the creation of effective schools (Bryk and Schneider 2002). Working together, stakeholders promote higher-quality education, making the relationship between parents, students, teachers, and administrators more cooperative (Henig 1994).

Although evidence on the optimal scale of operations is limited, there is little doubt that these movements have been increasing. School consolidation may represent one of the most significant reforms in education governance and management in the United States in the 20th century (Tyack 1974). Despite a growing population, more than 100,000 school districts have been eliminated since 1938, a decline of nearly 90 percent (National Center for Education Statistics 2003). There are also a growing number of private school franchises and charter school partnerships and EMOs in the United States (Lips 2000). For instance, Edison Schools, the largest U.S. for-profit charter school management organization, has grown from slightly more than 200 charter schools in 1995 to more than 3,600 charter schools in 2006. The small schools movement has also made significant progress in recent years. For example, the Bill and Melinda Gates Foundation recently invested more than US$1 billion to divide large urban high schools in the United States. In 2002, these resources partly funded the creation of 197 small high schools in New York City alone.

Much of the existing empirical evidence has focused on the consequences of public school district consolidation and the division of large public school districts (Duncombe et al. 2006), and only a small number of studies have examined the benefits of school franchises (Gill et al. 2007) and small independent schools (American Institutes for Research [AIR] and Stanford Research Institute [SRI] International 2005). The empirical evidence is often clouded by methodological limitations. In their extensive review of the literature, Andrews and his colleagues (2002) conclude that "both the claims of supporters of consolidation and detractors that claim small is beautiful have not adequately been tested using good evaluation methods."

The research that examines the benefits of private school franchises versus small independent schools also suffers from thin data because it derives from the evaluation of small-scale programs. The empirical findings on the impact of these small-scale programs in the United States are mixed. For instance, in their evaluation of Edison Schools researchers find that the performance of these schools varies (Gill et al. 2007). Similarly, the evaluations of the small high schools funded by the Gates Foundation also suggest that there is wide variation in the quality of these schools (AIR and SRI 2005).

The evidence on private school franchises and small private independent schools is limited because there are only a few education systems that provide public funding to private schools (Organisation for Economic Co-operation and Development [OECD] 2003). We can gain insight into the distinct strands of arguments on the optimal size of schooling operations by examining school systems in which vouchers have been implemented on a large scale and in which private school supply has increased. In 1981, Chile began financing public and most private schools with vouchers. The reform sparked a redistribution of students across private and public schools, as well as the creation of many new private schools. Although many private voucher schools are run by religious organizations, most are operated by private entrepreneurs (Elacqua 2007). Private voucher schools currently account for more than 40 percent of total enrollment, and about one-third of these schools belong to private voucher school franchises. This chapter compares the achievement of fourth graders in private voucher school franchises, private voucher independent schools, and public schools in Chile.

This chapter is not the first attempt to compare private and public school achievement in Chile. Earlier work used school-level data (e.g., Bravo et al. 1999; Mizala and Romaguera 2000). More recently, researchers used student-level data and attempted to control for selection bias (e.g., Anand et al. 2006; Contreras 2002; Gallego 2006; McEwan 2001; Sapelli and Vial 2002). Most of these studies show a private school advantage, although the differences are usually small.[1]

This chapter differs from earlier work by examining achievement across private voucher schools according to their network size. We consider private voucher school franchises and private voucher independent schools that do not belong to a franchise; previous analysts have used a single category to describe all private schools, with the exception of McEwan (2001) and Elacqua (2007), who considered different categories of private schools, including Catholic, Protestant, and for-profit schools. The results presented in this study demonstrate the importance of going beyond aggregate private voucher school categories and provide suggestive evidence that, all else being equal, students at private school franchises earn higher scores than those attending private independent and public schools.

The rest of this chapter is organized as follows. The following section reviews some background on Chile's voucher program and describes the private school categories that we will use in the empirical analysis. That is followed by a section presenting the empirical strategy that will be used to compare student achievement across school categories and describing the data that will be used to implement it. The next section presents and interprets results, and the final section concludes and discusses policy implications.

Background on Chile

During the 1980s, the school system in Chile experienced a reform program instituted by the military government (1973–90). First, the government decentralized the administration of schools, transferring responsibility for public school management from the Ministry of Education to municipalities. Second, the government changed the financing scheme of public and private schools that did not charge tuition. Public schools continued to be funded centrally, but municipalities started to receive a per-student voucher for every child attending their schools. As a result, enrollment losses came to have a direct effect on their education budgets. Most important, private schools that did not charge tuition began receiving the same per-student voucher as the public schools. Tuition-charging private schools continued to operate mostly without public funding.

The reform sparked a redistribution of students across private and public schools, as well as the establishment of many new private voucher schools. In 1980, 14 percent of Chilean K–12 students attended private schools that received public funds, and another 6 percent attended more elite, unsubsidized private schools. By 1990, 34 percent of students attended private voucher schools, and by 2003 enrollment in such schools had reached almost 40 percent of total enrollment. Adding in the 9 percent of students in elite private nonvoucher schools[2] leaves a slight majority of Chilean students in public schools (see figure 2.1).

Finally, it is worth noting that the essential features of the per-pupil voucher system have remained in place for almost a quarter century. The center-left coalition in power since 1990 has chosen to focus on improving the quality of poor schools through direct resource investments, while maintaining the organizational and funding components introduced in the 1980s (OECD 2004).[3]

Most researchers generally use a single category to describe all private voucher schools in Chile. However, as we will demonstrate below, there is variation in the size of private voucher school operations. The data presented in table 2.1 suggest that the private voucher school sector is essentially a cottage industry. Almost 68 percent of private voucher schools are independent schools that do not belong to a franchise. Private voucher school franchises, which are defined in Chile as schools that belong to a

Figure 2.1   Enrollment Share in Public and Private Schools, 1979–2003

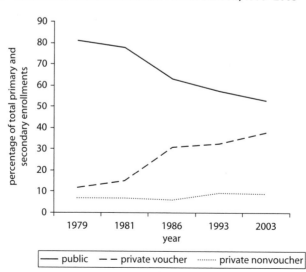

Source: Ministry of Education and authors' calculations.

Table 2.1   Distribution of Primary Schools and Students across Private Voucher School Categories, 2003

Number of schools in franchise	Share of schools	Share of enrollment	Average school size (number of students)	Percentage rural
Voucher 1 school	67.7	59.8	265	29
Voucher franchise 2 schools	12.1	13.1	314	29
Voucher franchise 3 schools	3.9	6.6	448	12
Voucher franchise 4 schools	1.9	3.1	481	11
Voucher franchise 5 schools	2.4	3.7	450	25
Voucher franchise >5 schools	12.0	13.7	311	4
Total	100	100	293	29
Number of schools or students	2,872	914,439		

Source: Ministry of Education and authors' calculations.

network of schools operated by the same "owner" (*sostenedor*), account for a little more than one-third of private voucher schools and enrollments. Most of the franchises are fairly small in scale, and only about 20 percent of primary private voucher students attend schools that belong to franchises that have more than three schools. Franchises are larger than private independent schools and less likely to be located in rural areas as the franchise size expands.

Empirical Strategy

In this section, we describe an empirical strategy for comparing student achievement at private independent schools and at private franchise and public schools, accounting for selection bias. Our empirical model builds on previous work by McEwan (2001).[4]

We hypothesize that student achievement, measured as student performance on standardized tests, can be modeled as a function of student socioeconomic characteristics (family background, home resources, and peer groups[5]). In this chapter, we have one public school category and six categories of private voucher schools. The sample is divided among school categories because we estimate separate regression coefficients for each subsample.

We can then predict the achievement of a "typical" student in each school category and subtract one prediction from another to measure the difference in achievement. We compare all school categories with the private independent voucher schools, which we use as a benchmark. For example, the (corrected) difference between private franchise voucher schools and private independent voucher schools provides an approximation of the expected increase (or decrease) in test scores for the average private independent school student if she were to attend a private franchise voucher school. However, a simple comparison of student outcomes in private franchise and private independent schools is unlikely to give unbiased estimates of the impact of private schools on student achievement.

Following McEwan (2001), we hypothesize that a person's probability of choosing a given school type is affected by the number of schools of each type per square kilometer in the person's municipality. All else being equal, students are more likely to choose schooling alternatives that are more densely concentrated in their municipalities.[6] It is assumed, however, that school densities are not correlated with student achievement.[7] Thus, school choice is influenced by local school supply, but school densities at the community level do not influence individual achievement.

There are reasons to doubt that assumption. We acknowledge that much of the debate on differences between public and private schools has revolved around statistical techniques that purport to control for student background characteristics and for potential selection on unobserved variables (e.g., Vandenberghe and Robin 2004). As was mentioned before, rather than developing a different empirical strategy to control for selection bias, our empirical model builds on previous published work by McEwan (2001) that uses the same student-level data in Chile. This will allow us to compare outcomes across private school types.

Data

The models in this chapter are estimated with student data from Chile's national standardized test, Sistema de Medición de la Calidad de la Educación (the System of Measurement of the Quality of Education—SIMCE), which annually assesses students in grades 4, 8, and 10 in language, mathematics, history and geography, and natural sciences in odd years. In 2002 SIMCE evaluated 274,863 fourth graders. Student test scores are complemented with parent and teacher questionnaires, which include socioeconomic and environmental information on the students, their families, their peers, and their schools. Table 2.2 provides definitions of the dependent and independent variables used in the analysis. We use

Table 2.2   Variable Definitions

Variable	Description
SPANISH	Student score on the fourth grade Spanish test (standardized to a mean of 0 and a standard deviation of 1)
MATH	Student score on the fourth grade mathematics test (standardized to a mean of 0 and a standard deviation of 1)
FEMALE	Dummy variable indicating whether student is female
MTHSCH	Years of schooling of student's mother
MTHMISS	Dummy variable indicating whether MTHSCH is missing
FTHSCH	Years of schooling of student's father
FTHMISS	Dummy variable indicating whether FTHSCH is missing
INCOME	Monthly family income, divided by 100,000
BOOKS1-BOOKS8	Eight dummy variables indicating the number of books in the family home, ranging from 1 (5 or less) to 8 (more than 200). BOOKS2 is omitted in regressions.
AVMTHSCH	Average schooling of student mothers in classroom
AVFTHSCH	Average schooling of student fathers in classroom
AVINCOME	Average monthly household income of students in classroom
TUITION	Average monthly tuition (in Chilean pesos) for students in school
SCHOOLSIZE	Total enrollment in school
SCHOOLSKM2	Number of schools per square kilometer
SECPROPORTION	Proportion of secondary students over total enrollment
RURAL	Dummy variable indicating whether school is rural

Source: Authors.

as dependent variables SPANISH and MATH, which were standardized to a mean of 0 and a standard deviation of 1.

Several independent variables characterize student demographics. These include the student's gender (FEMALE), years of parental schooling (MTHSCH and FTHSCH), self-reported household income (INCOME), and the number of non-school-related books in the student's home (BOOKS1-BOOKS8, expressed as a series of dummy variables). We imputed missing parent education information using student peer characteristics. A set of dummy variables (MTHMISS and FTHMISS) is included to identify those observations with imputed data.

We calculated student peer information by averaging individual student information over all students in a given classroom. AVMTHSCH and AVFTHSCH provide measures of the average parental schooling, and AVINCOME is the average household income in each classroom.

We also include a measure of average monthly tuition charged (TUITION),[8] a variable to indicate the relative isolation of the school (RURAL), and the total number of students enrolled at the school (SCHOOLSIZE).[9] Although they were not reported in the subsequent analysis, we also included regional dummy variables—relative to the metropolitan region—in the regressions to account for differences across regions. To approximate the number of neighborhood schooling options a family confronts, we include a measure of the number of schools in each category per square kilometer in each municipality (SCHOOLSKM2). A variable indicating the proportion of total enrollment in secondary school (SECPROPORTION) is also included.

Table 2.3 provides descriptive statistics for the 252,202 students that make up the sample, divided by school category. The distribution across school categories in the sample is similar to the universe of primary enrollments (see table 2.1). According to table 2.3, excluding private non-voucher schools, 58 percent of total enrollment is in public schools and the other 42 percent of students attend private voucher schools. The data presented in table 2.3 also show that 58 percent of the private voucher school students attend independent schools that do not belong to a franchise.

Empirical Results

A brief summary of the differences between results for both public and franchise schools as compared with private independent voucher schools is provided in table 2.4, under a broad set of control variables and corrections for selection bias. The table is divided into two panels. The top panel summarizes the results for Spanish, and the bottom presents the results for mathematics. The first row presents the unadjusted difference in test scores between public and franchise voucher schools, and private independent voucher schools.[10] The next row presents the differences after accounting for individual and peer attributes and selection bias.

The unadjusted estimates in table 2.4 suggest that students in private franchise voucher schools of any size have higher Spanish achievement than private voucher independent students. For example, the uncorrected advantage of private voucher schools that belong to a franchise of two schools is more than 0.03 standard deviations. Private students that attend schools that belong to a franchise of three or more schools score, on average, more than 0.16 standard deviations higher than private voucher independent students. Raw differences on the mathematics test are similar, but the gaps are slightly narrower.

Now consider the effects of each school category in Spanish and mathematics achievement, correcting for student and peer variables and selection bias. Three categories of schools have positive and significant effects on Spanish achievement: private voucher franchises with three schools

Table 2.3 Sample Descriptive Statistics

			Voucher franchise size					
	Sample	*Public*	*1 school*	*2 schools*	*3 schools*	*4 schools*	*5 schools*	*>5 schools*
SPANISH	0.00	−0.16	0.16	0.19	0.38	0.45	0.33	0.37
	(1.00)	(0.98)	(1.00)	(0.98)	(0.92)	(0.98)	(0.93)	(0.96)
MATH	0.00	−0.15	0.15	0.20	0.31	0.43	0.32	0.33
	(1.00)	(0.99)	(0.99)	(0.98)	(0.93)	(1.01)	(0.96)	(0.98)
Public	0.58							
Voucher 1	0.24							
Voucher 2 franchise	0.06							
Voucher 3 franchise	0.03							
Voucher 4 franchise	0.01							
Voucher 5 franchise	0.01							
Voucher >5 franchise	0.06							
FEMALE	0.49	0.48	0.48	0.50	0.54	0.46	0.47	0.55
MTHSCH	10.68	10.68	10.68	10.68	10.68	10.68	10.68	10.68
	(3.70)	(3.70)	(3.70)	(3.70)	(3.70)	(3.70)	(3.70)	(3.70)
MTHMISS	0.11	0.11	0.10	0.10	0.10	0.09	0.09	0.09
FTHSCH	10.71	9.94	11.73	11.63	12.20	12.09	11.88	11.85
	(3.65)	(3.61)	(3.46)	(3.39)	(3.14)	(3.38)	(3.29)	(3.42)
FTHMISS	0.14	0.15	0.13	0.13	0.12	0.12	0.12	0.12
INCOME	2.45	2.02	3.05	2.97	3.17	3.42	2.98	3.00
	(2.16)	(1.73)	(2.58)	(2.45)	(2.42)	(3.08)	(2.25)	(2.41)
BOOKS1	0.17	0.22	0.10	0.11	0.07	0.08	0.09	0.10
BOOKS2	0.21	0.25	0.17	0.17	0.14	0.15	0.16	0.16
BOOKS3	0.22	0.22	0.21	0.22	0.22	0.19	0.21	0.21

(continued)

Table 2.3 Sample Descriptive Statistics (Continued)

	Sample	Public			Voucher franchise size			
			1 school	2 schools	3 schools	4 schools	5 schools	>5 schools
BOOKS4	0.20	0.17	0.24	0.24	0.26	0.25	0.26	0.25
BOOKS5	0.11	0.08	0.15	0.14	0.17	0.15	0.14	0.16
BOOKS6	0.04	0.03	0.05	0.05	0.06	0.07	0.06	0.05
BOOKS7	0.02	0.01	0.03	0.03	0.03	0.04	0.03	0.03
BOOKS8	0.04	0.02	0.05	0.05	0.05	0.07	0.05	0.05
RURAL	0.13	0.18	0.05	0.06	0.02	0.02	0.09	0.07
MTHSCH (peer)	10.70	9.94	11.70	11.57	12.13	12.14	11.95	11.91
	(1.84)	(1.46)	(1.83)	(1.79)	(1.34)	(1.99)	(1.44)	(1.69)
FTHSCH (peer)	10.73	9.97	11.74	11.64	12.22	12.08	11.91	11.87
	(1.89)	(1.53)	(1.88)	(1.81)	(1.34)	(2.06)	(1.48)	(1.76)
HH Income (peer)	2.44	2.02	3.04	2.96	3.16	3.41	2.97	2.99
	(1.19)	(0.69)	(1.51)	(1.36)	(1.13)	(2.01)	(1.10)	(1.28)
SCHOOLSIZE	794.8	718.1	780.5	1069.1	1679.6	965.3	901.00	862.4
	(689.2)	(468.1)	(671.8)	(1204.2)	(1909.9)	(457.2)	(432.1)	(525.0)
SECPROPORTION	0.08	0.04	0.13	0.11	0.17	0.13	0.14	0.13
	(0.15)	(0.12)	(0.17)	(0.16)	(0.16)	(0.15)	(0.15)	(0.17)
Lambda	0.55	0.21	0.73	1.40	1.55	1.77	1.76	1.31
	(0.65)	(0.19)	(0.55)	(0.75)	(0.89)	(0.88)	(1.00)	(0.76)
N (students)	252,202	147,197	60,686	15,044	6,876	3,082	3,107	16,210
N (schools)	5,574	3,439	1,391	260	98	40	49	297
N (franchises)	1713	n/a	1391	166	39	12	12	22

Source: Ministry of Education and authors' calculations.

Table 2.4   Differences between Results for Both Public and Franchise Schools as Compared with Private Independent Voucher Schools

		Voucher franchise size				
	Public	2 schools	3 schools	4 schools	5 schools	> 5 schools
SPANISH						
Unadjusted	**−0.335**	**0.026**	**0.163**	**0.176**	**0.162**	**0.203**
difference	[0.005]	[0.010]	[0.013]	[0.017]	[0.019]	[0.009]
Individual						
SES/peer	**−0.142**	0.143	**0.238**	0.201	**0.502**	**0.227**
SES/selectivity	[0.047]	[0.084]	[0.077]	[0.226]	[0.135]	[0.066]
Number of						
observations	108,722	10,822	5,947	3,176	2,341	12,311
MATH						
Unadjusted	**−0.309**	**0.047**	**0.111**	**0.188**	**0.157**	**0.181**
difference	[0.005]	[0.010]	[0.013]	[0.017]	[0.019]	[0.009]
Individual						
SES/peer	−0.067	**0.202**	**0.367**	0.393	**0.364**	**0.344**
SES/selectivity	[0.049]	[0.084]	[0.086]	[0.207]	[0.174]	[0.078]
Number of						
observations	108,911	10,846	5,947	3,179	2,346	12,318

Source: Ministry of Education and authors' calculations.
Note: Standard errors are in parentheses. All regression results cluster standard errors at the school level.

(0.24), five schools (0.50), and five or more schools (0.23). The adjusted effects on mathematics achievement are similar, but the differences are larger for students that attend private voucher franchises with three schools (0.37) and more than five schools (0.34),[11] are statistically significant for two schools (0.20), and smaller for five schools (0.36). The corrected test score estimates also indicate that there is no significant difference in mathematics achievement between private independent voucher and public schools.

Are the magnitudes of these effects substantial? We used student-level test score data and the same empirical strategy as McEwan (2001) to correct for student and peer attributes and selection bias. Thus it may be useful to compare our findings. First, McEwan (2001) finds that there is no important difference in achievement between public and nonreligious private voucher schools. We find a small difference in student achievement between public and private independent voucher schools. McEwan (2001) also demonstrates that Catholic voucher schools have an advantage over most public and private voucher schools, once student and peer attributes and selection bias are accounted for. He estimates that Catholic schools in Chile have an effect size of about 0.09 standard deviations. We find that schools that belong to a franchise have even more substantial effect sizes, on average nearly one-third of a standard deviation.

Conclusion

This chapter compares the academic achievement of fourth graders in private voucher school franchises, public schools, and private independent voucher schools. Controlling for individual and peer characteristics, the initial results suggest that a representative private independent voucher student would achieve higher in private voucher franchise schools, relative to private independent voucher schools. Achievement is about 0.13 of a standard deviation higher. Students in private independent voucher schools—by far the largest category of private voucher schools—have slightly higher test scores than public school students.

When comparing with independent private voucher schools, controlling for selection bias significantly reduced the disadvantage of public schools and increased the advantage of private franchise schools.

We also considered the size of the private voucher school franchises. We found that, after controlling for individual and peer characteristics and selection bias, students in larger private school franchises outperform their private independent school peers. Achievement is more than 0.10 of a standard deviation higher on the Spanish and mathematics tests.

Some reasons that may explain the positive private school franchise effect include the substantial benefits of scale of education professionals and administrators (Chubb 2001), the bulk purchases of supplies and equipment, and the costs of implementing innovations in the curriculums (Duncombe and Yinger 2005). Private school franchises may also be more likely to benefit from access to credit and private investment than smaller independent private schools in Chile. In addition, some argue that being embedded in a larger communal organization reduces agency problems and facilitates transactions among parents, teachers, administrators, and students (McMeekin 2003) and influences the development of professional school communities (Bulkley and Hicks 2003; Smith and Wohlstetter 2001).

Before holding these results up as proof that private school franchises are more effective than private independent schools, we need additional information on the factors that may influence a school owner to establish a franchise. For instance, high-achieving schools may be more likely to establish franchises (or to join a franchise) than are low-quality schools.

In a competitive schooling environment, low-quality schools may be unable to attract students and additional resources needed to expand operations. Private school franchises may also require superior technical skills to manage compared with skills required to manage small independent schools. An instrumental variable, which may allow us to identify such causal effects, is a topic for future research.[12]

Further research for a high-quality research agenda in Chile will include at least four aspects. First, future work should attempt to model the choice of school owners to join a franchise or to add a school to their network. An alternative would be to use school panel data to examine how networks are created over time.

Second, unlike other voucher programs in other countries, private schools in Chile can choose their students.[13] However, public schools are prohibited from shaping their pool of students, except in cases in which schools are oversubscribed. Literature using Chilean data has practically omitted this important issue. However, the emerging legislation in Chile may exert stricter control over school admission procedures, providing leverage to identify more credible causal effects.

Third, a new institutional arrangement will be established in Chile. Policy makers are currently designing a public agency responsible for the quality of education. This agency will be responsible for monitoring the outcomes of the different types of schools and their academic performance and will have the authority to close schools and relocate students to other schools. This is an important topic for future research.

Finally, most of the interventions in education in Chile are applied universally. Many researchers have been promoting more randomization in programs. In other words, given the significant resources allocated to education, to better identify the relative success of different policies and programs, researchers and policy makers need to conduct randomized pilot studies.

From a policy perspective, the results of this study also suggest that more information is needed on the factors that influence schools' incentives to establish franchises. For instance, how profitable are private school franchises? The data presented in table 2.1 reveal that almost two-thirds of private voucher schools do not belong to a franchise. Small private independent schools may not have incentives to establish a franchise if they are able to attract enough students and resources to cover the opportunity costs of operating a school. Anecdotal evidence in Chile suggests that many of the independent private voucher school owners are former public school teachers.[14] Therefore, the opportunity cost of running a private voucher school, in many cases, may only be a public school teacher's salary after covering operational costs. Data on the characteristics of school owners would improve our understanding of the complex decisions involved in establishing a private school franchise.

The results of this chapter offer some insights for the debate in the United States on school vouchers, on the scale of operations of public and charter schools, and on the benefits of EMOs that manage several schools in a network. The findings provide some ground for optimism about the effects of school vouchers and some (but not all) categories of private schools on student achievement. Perhaps the most interesting finding of this research is the positive differences in achievement between private franchised voucher schools and private independent voucher schools. This suggests that policies oriented to create incentives for schools to establish franchises, or to be managed by an organization that runs a network of schools, may have the potential for increasing education outcomes.

Notes

1. There is also a vigorous debate on whether 25 years of vouchers in Chile has improved student achievement. For instance, Hsieh and Urquiola (2006) found that in Chile competition is not associated with higher public school performance because, according to the authors, private voucher schools responded to the competitive pressures let loose under the voucher system, not by raising productivity, but rather by choosing better students. Conversely, Gallego (2006) found that greater competition is associated with higher student achievement.

2. We do not include the private nonvoucher schools in this analysis. This set of schools charges high tuition, does not receive per-pupil subsidies, and is focused mainly on high-income students. In a previous version of the paper that this chapter is based on we included private nonvoucher schools in our analysis. The results (available on request) do not change the substantive conclusions reported here.

3. The only significant modification was in 1994, when the Ministry of Education instituted a shared financing scheme that allowed all private voucher schools—both elementary and secondary—and public secondary schools to charge limited tuition (Montt et al. 2006).

4. For a more technical discussion of our empirical strategy, see the working paper, which is available on request.

5. We include peer group controls because a body of literature has documented the positive spillover effects of having high-ability peers and the negative effects of being surrounded by disadvantaged students (e.g., Zimmer and Toma 2000).

6. Municipalities are recognized neighborhoods in Chile around which many services are organized. Municipalities are important in how people think about neighborhoods and how services are organized—that is, they have both a social reality in defining neighborhoods and a political reality in defining public services (see, for example, Valenzuela 1997). More than 80 percent of primary school students go to school in their home municipality. Thus, the density measure provides a good proxy for local neighborhood schooling options.

7. The regression results are available on request.

8. In 1994, the Ministry of Education instituted a shared financing scheme that allowed all private voucher schools—both elementary and secondary—and public secondary schools to charge limited tuition (Montt et al. 2006).

9. The size of the school has a positive and statistically significant effect on a child's Spanish test scores for four of the school categories, positive and not significant for two, and negative and significant for one of the school types. This variable has a positive and significant effect on a student's mathematics test score for three of the school categories, positive and not significant for three, and negative for one.

10. We use private independent schools as the omitted reference category because we are interested in comparing private franchise and independent school outcomes.

11. In a separate analysis not reported here, we excluded the largest private voucher school franchise in Chile, which has 147 schools, to make sure it was not confounding our findings. The results (available on request) do not change the substantive conclusions reported here.

12. Another topic for future research, which is beyond the scope of this chapter, is to compare the effectiveness of smaller and larger public school districts (*municipalidades*).

13. For example, in the Netherlands and Belgium the private sector plays a significant role in education. However, schools are not permitted to select students.

14. An official at the National Private Voucher School Association provided us with this information.

References

AIR (American Institutes for Research) and SRI (Stanford Research Institute) International. 2005. *National Evaluation of the Early College High School Initiative.* Bill & Melinda Gates Foundation, Seattle, WA.

Anand, P., A. Mizala, and A. Repetto. 2006. "Using School Scholarships to Estimate the Effect of Government Subsidized Private Education on Academic Achievement in Chile." National Center for the Study of

Privatization in Education Occasional Paper 120. Teachers College, Columbia University, New York.

Andrews, M., W. Duncombe, and J. Yinger. 2002. "Revisiting Economies of Size in American Education: Are We Any Closer to a Consensus?" *Economics of Education Review* 21 (3): 245–62.

Barker, R. G., and P. V. Gump. 1964. *Big School, Small School: High School Size and Student Behavior.* Stanford, CA: Stanford University Press.

Belfield, C., and H. Levin. 2005. "Vouchers and Public Policy: When Ideology Trumps Evidence." *American Journal of Education* 111 (2005): 548–67.

Belfield, C., and H. M. Levin. 2005. *Privatizing Educational Choice: Consequences for Parents, Schools, and Public Policy.* London: Paradigm Publishers.

Bravo, D., D. Contreras, and C. Sanhueza. 1999. "Educational Achievement, Inequalities and Private/Public Gap: Chile 1982–1997." Mimeo. Departamento de Economía, Universidad de Chile, Santiago.

Brown, H., J. Henig, N. Lacireno-Paquet, and T. Holyoke. 2004. "Scale of Operations and Locus of Control in Market- versus Mission-Oriented Charter Schools." *Social Science Quarterly* 85 (5): 1035–51.

Bryk, A., and B. Schneider. 2002. *Trust in Schools: A Core Resource for Improvement.* New York: Russell Sage Foundation.

Bulkley, K., and J. Hicks. 2003. "Educational Management Organizations and the Development of Professional Community in Charter Schools." National Center for the Study of Privatization in Education Occasional Paper 69. National Center for the Study of Privatization in Education, Teachers College, Columbia University, New York.

Chubb, J. E. 2001. "The Profit Motive. The Private Can Be Public." *Education Next* 1 (1).

Contreras, D. 2002. "Vouchers, School Choice and the Access to Higher Education." Center Discussion Paper 845. Economic Growth Center, Yale University, New Haven, CT.

Duncombe, W., and J. Yinger. 2005. "Does School District Consolidation Cut Costs?" Center for Policy Research at Syracuse University, Syracuse, NY.

———. 2007. "Does School District Consolidation Cut Costs?" *Journal of Education Policy and Finance* 4 (2): 341–76.

Elacqua, G. 2007. "The Politics of Education Reform in Chile: When Ideology Trumps Evidence." Presented at the Latin American Studies Association Annual Conference, Montreal, Canada.

Gallego, F. 2006. "Voucher School Competition, Incentives, and Outcomes: Evidence from Chile." Unpublished PhD dissertation. Massachusetts Institute of Technology, Cambridge.

Gill, B, R. Zimmer, J. Christman, and S. Blanc. 2007. "State Takeover, School Restructuring, Private Management, and Student Achievement in Philadelphia." Rand Corporation, Washington, DC.

Henig, J. 1994. *Rethinking School Choice: Limits of the Market Metaphor.* Princeton, NJ: Princeton University Press.

Hill, P., L. Pierce, and J. Guthrie. 1997. "Reinventing Public Education: How Contracting Can Transform America's Schools" (RAND research study). Chicago, IL: University of Chicago Press.

Hoxby, C. 1994. "Do Private Schools Provide Competition for Public Schools?" NBER Working Paper 4978. Available at SSRN: http://ssrn.com/abstract=226577.

Hsieh, C. T., and M. Urquiola. 2006. "The Effects of Generalized School Choice on Achievement and Stratification: Evidence from Chile's School Voucher Program." *Journal of Public Economics* 90 (8–9): 1477–1503.

Lee, V. E., and S. Loeb. 2000. "School Size in Chicago Elementary Schools: Effects on Teachers' Attitudes and Students' Achievement." *American Educational Research Journal* 37 (1): 3–31.

Lips, C. 2000. "'Edupreneurs': A Survey of For-Profit Education." Cato Policy Analysis No. 386. Cato Institute, Washington, DC.

McEwan, P. 2001. "The Effectiveness of Public, Catholic, and Non-Religious Private Schools in Chile's Voucher System." *Education Economics* 9 (2): 103–28.

McMeekin, R. 2003. "Networks of Schools." *Education Policy Analysis Archives* 11 (16).

Mizala, A., and P. Romaguera. 2000. "School Performance and Choice: The Chilean Experience." *Journal of Human Resources* 35 (2): 392–417.

Montt, P., G. Elacqua, P. Gonzalez, and D. Razyinski. 2006. "Hacia un sistema escolar descentralizado, sólido y fuerte: El diseño y las capacidades hacen la diferencia." Ministerio de Educación, Santiago, Chile.

National Center for Education Statistics. 2003. *Digest of Education Statistics, 2002.* U.S. Department of Education, Washington, DC.

OECD (Organisation for Economic Co-operation and Development). 2003. *Education at a Glance.* Paris: OECD.

———. 2004. *Revisión de políticas nacionales de educación: Chile.* Paris: OECD.

Palomer, C. G., and R. Paredes. 2006. Reducing the Educational Gap in Chile: Good Results in Vulnerable Groups. Working paper. PUC, Chile.

Raywid, M. A. 1998. "Small Schools: A Reform That Works." *Educational Leadership* 55 (4): 34–39.

Sapelli, C., and B. Vial. 2002. The Performance of Private and Public Schools in the Chilean Voucher System. *Cuadernos de Economía* 39 (118): 423–54.

Schneider, M., P. Teske, and M. Marschall. 2000. *Choosing Schools*. Princeton, NJ: Princeton University Press.

Smith, A., and P. Wohlstetter. 2001. "Reform through School Networks: A New Kind of Authority and Accountability." *Educational Policy* 15 (4): 499–519.

Steifel. L., R. Berne, P. Iatarola, and N. Fruchter. 2000. "High School Size: Effects on Budgets and Performance in New York City." *Educational Evaluation and Policy Analysis* 22 (1): 22–39.

Tyack, D. 1974. *The One Best System: A History of American Urban Education*. Cambridge, MA: Harvard University Press.

Valenzuela, J. P. 1997 "Descentralización Fiscal: Los ingresos municipales y regionales en Chile." *Política Fiscal Series*, ECLAC.

Vandenberghe, V., and S. Robin. 2004. "Evaluating the Effectiveness of Private Education across Countries: A Comparison of Methods." *Labour Economics* 11 (4): 487–506.

Wasley, P. M., M. Fine, N. E. Gladden, S. P. Holland, E. King, E. Mosak, and L. C. Powell. 2000. "Small Schools: Great Strides. A Study of New Small Schools in Chicago." http://www.essentialschools.org/cs/resources/view/ces_res/19. Accessed March, 17, 2007.

Whittle, C. I. 2000. "Winners of This Race Are Children." *Business Week*, February 7 (www.businessweek.com/2000/00_06/b3667005.htm).

Wohlstetter, P., C. Malloy, G. Hentschke, and J. Smith. 2004. "Improving Service Delivery in Education through Collaboration: An Exploratory Study of the Role of Cross-Sectoral Alliances in the Development and Support of Charter Schools." *Social Science Quarterly* 85 (5): 1078–96.

Zimmer, R. W., and E. F. Toma. 2000. "Peer Effects in Private and Public Schools across Countries." *Journal of Policy Analysis and Management* 19 (1): 75–92.

CHAPTER 3

Returns to Schooling and Vouchers in Chile

Harry Anthony Patrinos and Chris Sakellariou

Introduction

In 1981 Chile took bold steps to reform the education system. The introduction of school choice and decentralization of services was universal and rapidly implemented. The reform led to a new role for the state in education. The incentives led to a new role for the private sector, as a provider, and its share in the education system grew dramatically. The subject of school choice is still controversial—in Chile and abroad—and much has been written on the subject. Here, to analyze the true relationship between education attainment and labor market outcomes, we focus on the dramatic increases in enrollments in schooling that coincided with the rollout of the reforms. Secondary school expansion in the 1980s was impressive, and the system was able to absorb and retain many more students who otherwise would not have gone on to secondary schooling. Private school expansion helped absorb many of the new students. We exploit the 1981 reform to estimate more precise returns to schooling

The views expressed in this paper should not be attributed to the World Bank Group. The authors thank Emiliana Vegas for comments and support, as well as Felipe Barrera-Osorio, Eric Bettinger, Erik Bloom, Marco Manacorda, and seminar participants in Washington, DC, and London, UK.

using a special survey that includes cognitive skills. We use the large shift of students to the private subsidized schools. It is precisely these "switchers" that allow us to undertake this analysis. We find that the 1981 reform helped make the system more efficient, incorporating more students, at lower cost to the public sector.

When returns to schooling are estimated using a Mincer-type earnings function, the disturbance term will capture individual unobservable attributes and effects that, in general, tend to influence the schooling decision, hence resulting in a correlation between schooling and the error term. If schooling is endogenous, then estimation by ordinary least squares (OLS) will yield biased estimates of the return to schooling. We avoid this problem by using a special survey that includes information on cognitive abilities.

The return to investing in education, based on past empirical studies, is known to differ among individuals with different cognitive skills. For example, evidence from the United States (Ingram and Neumann 2006) shows that during the past decades, individuals with college education but without specific skills—as measured by cognitive ability revealed by tests—experienced the lowest benefits from investing in education. Therefore, individuals with low ability may not benefit as much from investing in education, compared with individuals in the upper part of the ability distribution. For the latter, ability is expected to interact positively with education, resulting in higher benefits from education investments. The effect of introducing ability/skills differences is two pronged. First, the more able individuals may be able to "convert" schooling into human capital more efficiently than the less able, and that raises the return to schooling for the more able. In this case, it can be concluded that ability and education are complementing each other in producing human capital. However, the more able may have higher opportunity costs because they may have been able to earn more in the labor market, if ability to progress in school is positively correlated with the ability to earn, and this reduces the rate of return to schooling (Harmon and Walker 2000). Given a distribution of wages, having controlled for cognitive skills, we assume that this distribution reflects the distribution of inherent (noncognitive) unobserved ability. As a result, lower-ability individuals predominate in the lower quantiles of the distribution and higher-ability individuals predominate in the upper quantiles of the distribution.

When a true measure of ability is an omitted variable in the earnings equation, one of three different approaches has been used in the empirical literature to capture the "true" return to education. The first approach uses twins to arrive at a measure of the causal return to education. For example, Ashenfelter and Rouse (1998) and Rouse (1997) using data from the United States, have compared the earnings of twins with different education levels and reported an estimate of the return to education that is about 30 percent smaller than the OLS estimate. The second approach uses achievement test scores measuring cognitive ability and employs them as additional controls in the earnings function. The third approach uses sources for exogenous variation in education attainment, such as institutional changes in the schooling system in the form of changes in compulsory schooling laws and abolition of fees, as well as other "natural variations" (for example, school construction projects) affecting the schooling decision, to estimate a causal return to education effect using instrumental variable estimation.

Most estimates of the return to education based on "natural experiments" report a higher return to education (rather than a lower one), compared with OLS-based estimates of the return to education (see, for example, Angrist and Krueger 1991; Card 1995; Harmon and Walker 1995; Kane and Rouse 1993; Meghir and Palme 2005; for developing countries, see Duflo 1998; Patrinos and Sakellariou 2005; Sakellariou 2006). Many researchers believe that typical estimates that do not control for ability bias significantly overstate the true causal effect of education on earnings. Thus, they would argue that findings to the contrary are counterintuitive. The dominant explanation for these results is that institutional changes in the school system (such as compulsory schooling laws) affect the schooling decision of a subset of individuals who otherwise would not have pursued a higher level of education, not the average individual. Furthermore, individuals affected by such reforms tend to have a higher return to education than the average individual.

To incorporate cognitive ability, we rely on the Chilean data from the International Adult Literacy Survey (IALS).[1] The IALS was created to generate comparable literacy profiles across national, linguistic, and cultural boundaries. The IALS data have been used in several studies, with little evidence on Chile, the only country in the survey outside Europe and North America. Blau and Khan (2001) examined the role of cognitive skills in explaining higher wage inequality in the United States. Leuven et al. (2004) used IALS data for 15 countries (including Chile) and explored the hypothesis that wage differentials between skill groups across countries are consistent with a demand-and-supply framework. They find that cognitive achievement is an important determinant of earnings in all countries examined except Poland and Finland. They also find that about one-third of the variation in relative wages between skill groups across countries is explained by differences in net supply of skill groups. Green and Riddell (2002) used the measure of literacy in the IALS data set to examine the influence of cognitive and unobserved skills on earnings in Canada. They find that cognitive skills contribute significantly to earnings and that their inclusion in earnings equations reduces the measured impact of schooling. Their findings suggest that cognitive and unobserved skills are both productive but that having more of one skill does not enhance the other's productivity. Devroye and Freeman (2001) used the IALS survey and found that skill inequality among advanced countries explains only about 7 percent of the cross-country differences in earnings inequality. They also find that the bulk of cross-country differences in earnings inequality occur within skill groups, not between them.

We estimate the returns to schooling for those induced to make schooling decisions (involving quantity or quality) by the change associated with our instrument—the 1981 reform. In this study, the instrument corresponds to a policy of capitation grants that induced a group of individuals to opt for the opportunities that the policy made available. The estimates, therefore, identify a policy-relevant return to schooling in Chile.

The 1981 Vouchers Scheme

We estimate the causal effect of education on earnings by exploiting the school reform of 1981 to identify a binary instrument with and without controlling for cognitive skills. Chile, among developing countries, was a pioneer and has gone further than any other country to redefine the roles of the state and private sector in education by separating the financing from the provision of education. As a result of the capitation grants paid to schools and the opening of the education system to the private sector, Chile was able to absorb the pressure of secondary school expansion. There was a large shift of students to the private subsidized schools (mainly in major urban areas), whose enrollment increased by 93 percent between 1980 and 1985, at the expense of municipal schools. Despite a decline in public spending for education (from 4.0 percent of GDP in 1981 to 2.6 percent in 1990), student intake increased by 42 percent in higher education and by about 15 percentage points in secondary education (Delannoy 2000). As a result of the sweeping 1981 reform, the average years of schooling peak for the cohorts at about the time of and immediately after the reform.

Overall, the reform improved the efficiency of the education system. That is, the number of students educated per unit of public spending increased significantly during the 1980s. However, this was achieved at the expense of equity, as subsidized private schools serving a better informed, better-off population benefited from the opportunities offered by the capitation grants system at the expense of municipal schools that served the less-well-off section of the population.

The Chilean voucher system has been studied extensively. Some find that the voucher system had positive impacts on test scores and precollege examinations (Contreras and Macias 2002; Gallego 2002, 2004; Sapelli 2003; Sapelli and Vial 2002). Yet others find that there was no impact on test scores, repetition rates, or secondary school enrollment rates (Carnoy and McEwan 2000; Hsieh and Urquiola 2006). In addition, Gauri (1998) found that school choice had led to increased social and academic stratification. Bellei (2005) outlines three principal reasons that it is difficult to make comparisons between public and private schools in Chile and how they explain the widely diverging results in individual analyses, all stemming from the lack of random assignment of students to schools: (1) private schools tend to be located in urban areas and serve middle- to middle-high-income students; (2) there are wide differences in the level of resources available to schools, even among the same types of schools; and (3) there is very little information about how families select schools and how private schools select students. Thus, it is difficult to measure the supply of private schools and to control for school resources, and the estimates are riddled with selection bias. The studies also differ in the ways that they use control variables such as parental education, school socioeconomic status, student characteristics, test-score variation, and so on. Gallego (2006) explains that the differences in results can be attributed to changes in the voucher and education systems in the mid-1990s. Hoxby (2003) reiterates that existing studies lead to inconclusive evidence of impact because of a lack of random assignment, thus making it difficult to determine whether variation in school choice is endogenous, and because of a lack of pretreatment data. This chapter does not attempt to look at the impact of the reform in this light, but rather use the reform itself as an instrument to estimate the causal effect of education on earnings of the group affected by the 1981 education reform, as well as the effect of the reform on the quality of learning.

Who Is Affected by Education Reform?

The group affected by the education reform, although consisting of students with a variety of backgrounds, is expected to contain a large proportion of students from higher socioeconomic backgrounds and from urban areas. First, this is because in rural areas in Chile, low population density does not permit a choice of schools. Second, there is evidence that private subsidized schools tend to select students to a larger extent than do municipal schools (Contreras, Bustos, and Sepulveda 2007). Therefore, better private subsidized schools (as well as some elite municipal schools) that were facing excess demand practiced screening. According to Gauri (1998), 28 percent of students in the subsidized sector of Santiago had taken tests to be admitted in their current schools. Furthermore, top-up fees, lack of transparency in enrollment procedures, and the cost of uniforms constituted de facto screening devices. As a result, students who attend private subsidized schools come from higher-income and better educated families compared with students attending municipal schools (but not private nonsubsidized schools).

Instrumental variables (IV) estimates of the return to schooling are expected to differ from OLS estimates. Although the standard ability bias would suggest that the OLS estimates are biased upward, empirical evidence from using a variety of mainly binary instruments, several of which are based on education policy reforms, suggest that IV estimates are generally higher than OLS estimates. The dominant explanation for this (as given by Card 2001) is that because of heterogeneity, there is a distribution of returns, and OLS and IV estimates correspond to different weighted averages of this distribution. Therefore, IV estimates can exceed OLS estimates. The fact that the IV estimates are higher than the OLS estimates is interpreted as an indication that the return to the marginal person (the "switchers") is higher than that of the average person. Furthermore, Carneiro, Heckman, and Vytlacil (2005) show that the marginal person can have a return that is substantially lower than the return to the average person, and still the return estimate from IV is greater than the corresponding return from OLS.

Assuming that cognitive skills are associated with quality of schooling and that a group of students switched to better quality schools as a result of the reform, we would expect the affected group (especially those who switched to better quality schools at a younger age) to have higher and less dispersed cognitive skills. Therefore, the returns to cognitive skill scores in the IV regressions are expected to be lower compared with the OLS regressions.

The results from OLS regressions for returns to an additional year of schooling and the effects of controlling for the measure of cognitive skills using a sample composed of a group of 22- to 45-year-old males working for wages are presented in table 3.1. The dependent variable is the logarithm of hourly wage. Inclusion of the direct measure of cognitive ability reduces the return to schooling by about 34 percent; a one standard deviation increase in the score increases earnings by 17 percent. On average, the interaction effect of schooling with cognitive skills is moderately positive and nearly significant.

Table 3.2 presents results from IV regressions using the instrument based on the capitation grants reform. The binary instrument initially takes the value of 1 for those who at the time of the reform were 6 to 13 years old (22 to 29 years old in 1997—the year of the survey) and 0 otherwise, that is, those in the 8 years of basic education. One-third of the observations belong to the group affected by the reform. In the standard Mincerian specification, the IV estimate of the return to schooling is about 37 percent higher than the OLS estimate, and the assumption that the schooling variable is exogenous is rejected at the 5 percent level. Here the composition of the group affected by the reform needs to be considered. This group (which in this case consists of pupils in basic education) contains those who switched to private subsidized schools. Although there is no conclusive evidence in the literature that school choice improved the performance of the median student, it has been convincingly argued that the main effect of unrestricted school choice was an exodus of "middle class" students from public sector schooling (Hsieh and Urquiola 2006) and the practice of screening by private subsidized schools (competing for better students). Furthermore, it is possible that parents tended to select schools that provided good peer groups. On the basis of this evidence, we attribute the higher IV estimate of the return to schooling to those in a treated group with such characteristics, rather than to the average individual.

Without controlling for cognitive ability, cognitive ability will be part of the error term. The assumption of independence implies that the

Table 3.1   Returns to Schooling

	(1)	(2)	(3)	(4)
Average return to year of schooling	8.9	5.8	5.5	6.8
Controlling for skills	NO	YES	YES	YES
Interaction between skills and years of schooling	NO	NO	YES	NO
Father with upper secondary school	NO	NO	NO	YES

Source: Patrinos and Sakellariou 2008.
Note: From basic Mincerian earnings functions that include experience and experience-squared.

Table 3.2   Returns to Schooling Using 1981 Reform as Instrument

	(1)	(2)	(3)
Average return to year of schooling	**12.2**	**10.2**	**9.6**
Controlling for skills	NO	YES	YES
Interaction between skills and years of schooling	NO	NO	YES

Source: Patrinos and Sakellariou 2008.
Note: From basic Mincerian earnings functions that include experience and experience square.

instrument must be independent of cognitive ability. Therefore, when cognitive ability is not controlled for, the instrument is compromised. By controlling for cognitive ability we avoid the problem of using possibly invalid instruments and make our estimates more credible (Carneiro, Heckman, and Vytlacil 2005). When we include the measure of cognitive skills in the equation, the estimate of the return to schooling decreases by about 16 percent (which is much less than the reduction seen in the OLS regressions); the contribution of one standard deviation in the cognitive score to earnings is one-half the corresponding estimate from the OLS regressions. The results above seem to indicate that students who switched to private subsidized schools and in 1981 were of basic school age were part of a rather homogeneous group of students with above average cognitive skills. That is, "better" students formed the bulk of those who switched from public to private subsidized schools. As a result, only a small part of return to schooling estimate is due to classical ability bias. Column 3 indicates that the contribution of cognitive skills is mainly through their interaction with schooling (as was the case in the OLS regressions).

We further investigate the education-earnings relationship for a different age group. In table 3.3, the binary instrument is modified and takes the value of 1 for those who at the time of the reform were 6 to 18 years old (22 to 34 years old in 1997—the year of the survey) and 0 otherwise. That is, the group includes all those who could have been affected by the reform, either by switching to private subsidized schools because of their perceived higher quality compared with municipal schools, or by choosing to continue schooling at the secondary level as a result of the increase in the supply of private schools associated with the education reform, which led to a large increase in secondary school participation. Estimates of the return to schooling are now lower by 37 percent in the Mincerian specification and by more than 50 percent when we control for cognitive skills. At the same time, a one standard deviation increase in the cognitive

Table 3.3   Returns to Schooling Using 1981 Reform as Instrument, Males 22–45 Years Old

	(1)	(2)	(3)
Average return to year of schooling	7.7	4.3	4.2
Controlling for skills	NO	YES	YES
Interaction between skills and years of schooling	NO	NO	YES

Source: Patrinos and Sakellariou 2008.
Note: From basic Mincerian earnings functions that include experience and experience square.

score increases earnings by 20 percent, up from 8.5 percent. The coefficient estimates are now close to those from OLS; as a result the endogeneity test does not reject the null hypothesis that the difference in coefficients between IV and OLS is not systematic.

Finally, we ask the question, what happens if we progressively expand the treated group to include students who at the time of the reform were between the ages of 4 (20 years old in 1997) and 20 (36 years old in 1997)? That is, starting with a treated group of very young children in 1981 and progressively expanding the group one year at a time until age 20, tracing the changes coefficient estimates for schooling and cognitive skills. Suppose that such students, before deciding whether to switch schools (based on the comparison between expected benefits and costs) were enrolled in, say, municipal schools. Assuming that municipal schools on average provide lower-quality schooling, switching to private subsidized schools at a younger age (such as at the beginning of primary school) should result in a higher and more homogeneous cognitive skill endowment by the end of the schooling period, compared with switching at a later age (such as during high school). We, therefore, would expect that as we progressively increase the instrument upper cutoff age, the treated group becomes less endowed in cognitive skills (because they have received most of their schooling before 1981) and less homogeneous in these skills. As a result, as we add the marginal individual in the treated group, the return to cognitive skills will be increasing and the return to schooling will be decreasing. That is because part of a given estimate of the return to schooling from the Mincerian specification is due to the independent effect of cognitive skills. Given a group with less and more dispersed cognitive skills, a larger part of the Mincerian estimate of the return to schooling will be due to the independent effect of cognitive skills. The opposite is true for a group endowed with more and less dispersed cognitive skills.

Figure 3.1 confirms the hypothesis. The Mincerian return to schooling is 11 percent to 12 percent for the cohorts who in 1991 were of primary school age or lower; subsequently (by the end of basic education) the return declines sharply. In figure 3.2, the returns to schooling fluctuate at about 10 percent for the primary school cohorts and subsequently decline sharply. The opposite pattern is observed for the returns to cognitive score. With the last expansions of the instrument cutoff point, the return to schooling approaches zero; a one standard deviation increase in the cognitive score increases earnings by almost 30 percent. It can also be observed that the decline in the return to schooling estimate (increase in the return to cognitive score) coincides with the period between the end of the two cycles of compulsory basic education in Chile (ages 6–14) and the end of secondary education (ages 14–18).

Summarizing, the findings suggest that for a group of compliers who were of basic school age in 1981, about 84 percent of what the labor market rewarded was the noncognitive contribution of schooling. However, for the mixed group of compliers, which includes those who were of secondary school age, only about 56 percent of the labor market reward was for the noncognitive contribution of schooling.

Note, however, that when a measure of full cognitive skills is used, one cannot account for the origin of cognitive skills. For example, the IALS score used in this chapter measures an array of cognitive skills acquired by an individual, including skills acquired outside school (influenced mainly by the parental environment). Therefore, our earlier methodology assumes that all cognitive skills are acquired (or signaled) via schooling.

Figure 3.1   Returns to an Additional Year of Schooling for Different Instrument Cutoff Points

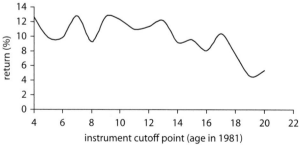

Source: Patrinos and Sakellariou 2008.

Figure 3.2   Returns to an Additional Year of Schooling and a One Standard Deviation Increase in Cognitive Ability, at Different Instrument Cutoff Points

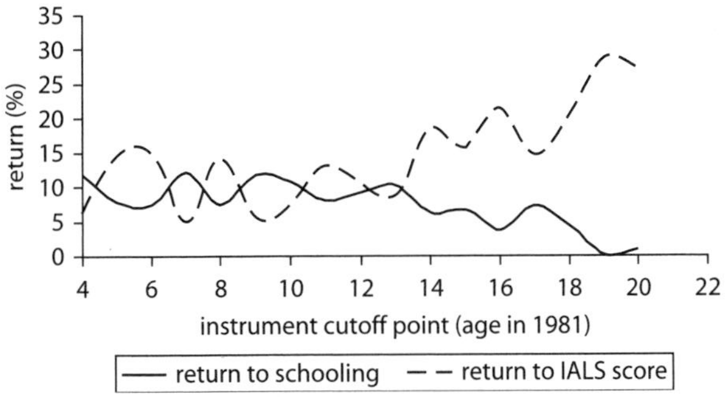

Source: Patrinos and Sakellariou 2008.

In what follows, we explore an alternative methodology in obtaining additional information about the relative size of the noncognitive versus cognitive components of the return to schooling. Following Ishikawa and Ryan (2002), Pasche (2007), and Tyler (2004), we develop a model for estimating cognitive and noncognitive components of the returns to schooling (for details see Patrinos and Sakellariou 2008). In table 3.4 we present the average marginal return to schooling from the standard specification, which is again about 9.0 percent. There is a significant decrease, of about 25 percent, in the average return to a year of schooling once we control for full cognitive skills. After controlling for both types of cognitive skills (column 4), both schooling and nonschooling cognitive skills are responsible for the overall decrease in the estimated return to a year of schooling. In this specification, schooling cognitive skills appear as more important. In fact, schooling cognitive skills are rewarded approximately 1.5 times more than nonschooling cognitive skills.

We incorporate skills in combination with the instruments in tables 3.5 and 3.6, effectively replicating table 3.4 using IV estimations. The third column replaces full cognitive skills with schooling cognitive skills; the fourth column includes "schooling" and "nonschooling cognitive skills." The findings in table 3.5 confirm the earlier conclusion that for this group of compliers, the coefficient of years of schooling is a measure mainly of the noncognitive return to schooling. The coefficient remains largely unchanged when we control separately for schooling cognitive skills and nonschooling cognitive skills, which enter the equation with coefficients that are statistically near zero.

Table 3.4   Average Returns to Schooling

	(1)	(2)	(3)	(4)
Average return to a year of schooling	9.0	6.8	7.6	6.9
Controlling for skills	NO	YES	–	–
Controlling for schooling cognitive skills	–	–	YES	YES
Controlling for nonschooling cognitive skills	–	–	NO	YES
Father has postsecondary+	YES	YES	YES	YES

Source: Patrinos and Sakellariou 2008.
Note: From basic Mincerian earnings functions that include experience and experience-squared.

Table 3.5   Returns to Schooling and Skills from IV, Male Employees 22–45 Years Old (for Sample That Was 6–13 Years of Age in 1981)

	(1)	(2)	(3)	(4)
Average return to a year of schooling	11.7	10.8	11.7	11.7
Controlling for full cognitive skills	NO .	YES	–	–
Controlling for schooling cognitive skills	–	–	YES	YES
Controlling for nonschooling cognitive skills	–	–	NO	YES
Father postsecondary+	YES	YES	YES	YES

Source: Patrinos and Sakellariou 2008.
Note: From basic Mincerian earnings functions that include experience and experience-squared.

Table 3.6   Returns to Schooling and Skills from IV, Male Employees 22–45 Years Old (for Sample That Was 6–18 Years of Age in 1981)

	(1)	(2)	(3)	(4)
Years of schooling	7.9	5.3	6.4	5.8
Controlling for full cognitive skills	–	YES	–	–
Controlling for schooling cognitive skills	–	–	YES	YES
Controlling for nonschooling cognitive skills	–	–	NO	YES
Father postsecondary+	YES	YES	YES	YES

Source: Patrinos and Sakellariou 2008.
Note: From basic Mincerian earnings functions that include experience and experience-squared.

Results in table 3.6 for the group of compliers of basic or secondary school age in 1981 are again drastically different. Overall, the IV estimates of the coefficient of years of schooling are now lower compared with the corresponding OLS estimates. Controlling for the two types of cognitive skills decreases the coefficient of years of schooling by about 27 percent compared with the standard specification in column 1. At the same time, one standard deviation increase in the score increases earnings by about 13 percent and 9 percent for schooling cognitive and nonschooling cognitive skills.

The evidence could be taken to suggest that the treated group that benefited most from the 1981 "voucher" reform, besides coming mainly from a better socioeconomic background and from urban areas, were enrolled in the early stages of schooling. They benefited from better quality schooling, which endowed them with better schooling cognitive skills (compared with the untreated). As a result, given the "abundance" of schooling cognitive skills in this group, the labor market reward for an additional year of schooling reflects the "true" noncognitive return to schooling.

However, the cohorts who obtained early childhood schooling before 1981 do not seem to have benefited as much. The reform facilitated the absorption of the large secondary school expansion, despite the decline in public spending for education. However, because of the secondary school expansion, lower-ability students (from "middle class" families or otherwise) may have been admitted into the system, students who had earlier received their basic education in public schools. This group entered the labor market less endowed in schooling cognitive skills. As a result, the labor marker rewarded these skills significantly; failure to control for such skills in the earnings function results in a return to schooling estimate that is seriously biased upward. The noncognitive component of the return to schooling for this group is rather small (about half that of the younger cohort).

The IV regressions using a treated group that consists of a mixture of basic and secondary-age students in 1981 result in estimates of gross returns as well as schooling returns with the cognitive skills component netted out; these estimates are smaller than the corresponding OLS estimates, at about 8 percent and 6 percent. However, comparing results using a treated group consisting of only basic school-age students with those using a mixture of basic and secondary age students in 1981 reveals considerable heterogeneity in the returns to schooling in Chile.

Conclusion

We use the sweeping school reform of 1981 in Chile to identify a binary instrument and estimate returns to schooling from IV, with and without controlling for cognitive ability. Given that ability bias needs to be dealt with, accounting for cognitive ability avoids the problem of using a possibly invalid instrument.

The 1981 capitation grant scheme facilitated the absorption of the pressure of secondary school expansion that resulted from the capitation grants paid to schools and the opening of the education system to the private sector and resulted in large increases in student intake as well as a sharp decline in the dropout rate, especially in basic education. Overall, the reform improved the efficiency of the education system, possibly at the expense of equity.

The results suggest that those who in 1981 switched to private subsidized schools were mainly urban "middle class" students leaving public schools, possibly in search of better peer groups. We find evidence suggesting that, for students with such characteristics who switched during their basic education, the labor market reward for an additional year of schooling is a measure of the noncognitive return to schooling. That is not the case, however, for older cohorts (those in secondary education). The large secondary school expansion seems to have attracted a heterogeneous group of students who had earlier received their basic education in public schools. For this group of students the labor marker rewarded these skills significantly, whereas the noncognitive component of the return to schooling for this group is rather small.

Note

1. For more details, see Patrinos and Sakellariou (2008).

References

Angrist, J., and A. Krueger. 1991. "Does Compulsory School Attendance Affect Schooling and Earnings?" *Quarterly Journal of Economics* 106 (4): 979–1014.

Ashenfelter, O., and C. E. Rouse. 1998. "Income, Schooling and Ability: Evidence from a New Sample of Identical Twins." *Quarterly Journal of Economics* 113 (1): 253–84.

Bellei, C. 2005. "The Private-Public School Controversy: The Case of Chile." Presented at the World Bank–Kennedy School of Government conference "Mobilizing the Private Sector for Public Education," Harvard University, Cambridge, MA. October 5–6.

Blau, F., and L. Khan. 2001. "International Differences in Male Wage Inequality: Institutions Versus Market Forces." *Journal of Political Economy* 104: 791–837.

Card, D. 1995. "Earnings, Schooling, and Ability Revisited." In *Research in Labor Economics*, ed. S. Polacheck. Greenwich, CT: JAI Press.

———. 2001. "Estimating the Return to Schooling: Progress on Some Persistent Econometric Problems." *Econometrica* 69.

Carneiro, P., J. Heckman, and E. Vytlacil. 2005. "Understanding What Instrumental Variables Estimate: Estimating Marginal and Average Returns to Education." University of Chicago, Department of Economics, Chicago, IL.

Carnoy, M., and P. McEwan. 2000. "The Effectiveness and Efficiency of Private Schools in Chile's Voucher System." *Educational Evaluation and Policy Analysis* 22 (3): 213–39.

Contreras, D., and V. Macias. 2002. "Competencia y Resultados Educacionales." University of Chile, Santiago.

Contreras, D., S. Bustos, and P. Sepulveda. 2007. "When Schools Are the Ones That Choose: the Effect of Screening in Chile." The World Bank, Washington, DC.

Delannoy, F. 2000. "Education Reforms in Chile, 1980–1998: A Lesson in Pragmatism." Education Reform and Management Publication Series, Volume 1, No. 1, World Bank, Washington, DC.

Devroye, D., and R. Freeman. 2001. "Does Inequality in Skills Explain Inequality of Earnings across Advanced Countries?" NBER (National Bureau of Economic Research) Working Paper 8140. NBER, Cambridge, MA.

Duflo, E. 1998. "Schooling and Labor Market Consequences of School Construction in Indonesia: Evidence from an Unusual Policy Experiment." *American Economic Review* 91 (4): 795–813.

Gallego, F. 2002. "Competencia y Resultados Educativos. Teoría y Evidencia para Chile." *Cuadernos de Economía* 39 (118): 309–52.

———. 2004. "School Choice, Incentives, and Academic Outcomes: Evidence from Chile." Massachusetts Institute of Technology, Cambridge, MA.

———. 2006. "Voucher-School Competition, Incentives and Outcomes: Evidence from Chile." Massachusetts Institute of Technology, Cambridge, MA.

Gauri, V. 1998. *School Choice in Chile. Two Decades of Educational Reform.* Pittsburgh, PA: Pittsburgh University Press.

Green, D., and C. Riddell. 2002. "Literacy and Earnings: An Investigation of the Interaction of Cognitive and Non-Cognitive Attributes in Earnings Generation." Discussion Paper 02-11. Department of Economics, University of British Columbia, Canada.

Harmon, C., and I. Walker. 1995. "Estimates of Economic Return to Schooling in the UK." Economics, Finance and Accounting Department Working Paper Series n540195. Department of Economics, Finance and Accounting, National University of Ireland, Maynooth.

———. 2000. "The Returns to the Quantity and Quality of Education: Evidence for Men in England and Wales." *Economica*, New Series 67(265): 19–35.

Hoxby, C. M. 2003. "School Choice and School Competition: Evidence from the United States." *Swedish Economic Policy Review* 10: 11–67.

Hsieh, C. T., and M. Urquiola. 2006. "The Effects of Generalized School Choice on Achievement and Stratification: Evidence from Chile's Voucher Program." *Journal of Public Economics* 90: 1477–1503.

Ingram, B., and G. Neumann. 2006. "The Returns to Skill." *Labour Economics* 13(1): 35–59.

Ishikawa, M., and D. Ryan. 2002. "Schooling, Basic Skills and Economic Outcomes." *Economics of Education Review* 21 (3): 231–43.

Kane, T., and T. Rouse. 1993. "Labor Market Returns to Two- and Four-Year Colleges: Is a Credit a Credit and Do Degrees Matter." NBER (National Bureau of Economic Research) Working Paper 4268. NBER, Cambridge, MA.

Leuven, E., H. Oosterbeek, and H. van Ophem. 2004. "Explaining International Differences in Male Skill Wage Differentials by Differences in Demand and Supply of Skills." *Economic Journal* 114: 466–86.

Meghir, C., and M. Palme. 2005. "Assessing the Effect of Schooling on Earnings Using a Social Experiment." *American Economic Review* 95 (1): 414–24.

Patrinos, H., and C. Sakellariou. 2005. "Schooling and Labor Market Impacts of a Natural Policy Experiment." *Labour* 19 (4): 705–19.

———. 2008. "Quality of Schooling, Returns to Schooling and the 1981 Vouchers Reform in Chile." Policy Research Working Paper Series 4617. World Bank, Washington, DC.

Pasche, C. 2007. "A New Measure of the Cognitive and Noncognitive Components of the Return to Schooling." University of Geneva, Switzerland. http://ssrn.com/abstract=983542.

Rouse, C. 1997. "Further Estimates of the Economic Return to Schooling from a New Sample of Twins." Princeton University, Princeton, NJ.

Sakellariou, C. 2006. "Education Policy Reform, Local Average Treatment Effect and Returns to Schooling from Instrumental Variables in the Philippines." *Applied Economics* 38: 473–81.

Sapelli, C. 2003. "The Chilean Voucher System: Some New Results and Research Challenges." *Cuadernos de Economía* 40 (121): 530–38.

Sapelli, C., and B. Vial. 2002. "The Performance of Private and Public Schools in the Chilean Voucher System." *Cuadernos de Economía* 39 (118): 423–54.

Tyler, J. 2004. "Basic Skills and the Earnings of Dropouts." *Economics of Education Review* 23 (3): 2121–235.

CHAPTER 4

When Schools Are the Ones That Choose: Policy Analysis of Screening in Chile

Dante Contreras, Sebastián Bustos, and Paulina Sepúlveda

Introduction

The international evidence convincingly demonstrates that education is a key factor for raising incomes, social mobility, and welfare.[1] From a theoretical point of view, there are at least three alternatives for obtaining better results. The first is to increase the resources spent on education. The empirical evidence indicates, however, that increasing the resources of the system does not necessarily lead to improved results.[2]

A second policy option is to introduce competition and incentive mechanisms through demand-side subsidies and vouchers. This system

The authors are grateful for the comments made by Felipe Barrera-Osorio, Sebastián Gallegos, Cristóbal Huneeus, Osvaldo Larrañaga, Karthik Muralidharan, Christopher Neilson, Valentina Paredes, Harry Patrinos, Claudia Sanhueza, and Pablo Serra. We are also indebted to the participants at the Seminar of the Department of Economics, Universidad de Chile, March 2007, and LACEA-LAMES 2007. This chapter is a summary of research distributed under the title "When Schools Are the Ones That Choose: The Effects of Screening in Chile." We would also like to express our gratitude to the funding provided by FONDECYT No. 1071123. Any error or omission is the sole responsibility of the authors.

uses direct subsidies allowing parents to choose. It is designed to encourage competition between education establishments in the provision of better education services to capture parents' preferences for their children's schooling.

The third alternative to improve education outcomes is to change incentives on the supply side. For instance, rewards to teachers based on performance, increases in schools' autonomy and accountability, and changes in teachers' wage structures.

A voucher system (the second alternative) was implemented in Chile in the early 1980s. Public and private subsidized schools receive a common direct subsidy from the government for each student admitted. If the student decides to change to another school, the new school receives the entire subsidy.

The Chilean experience is the most significant international example of a competition- and incentive-based education system. It is one of the few nationwide systems in the world and is backed by more than 20 years of data. Therefore, studying the Chilean case is crucial to evaluate the results of competition in a sector traditionally organized around classic public good mechanisms.[3]

The design above assumes the existence of an education market that operates as indicated. There are at least two characteristics of the Chilean system that call into question the functionality of this market. First, the evidence suggests that parents do not necessarily choose schools on the basis of quality, which is a key element for strengthening (weakening) good (bad) schools. In fact, Elacqua, Schneider, and Buckley (2006) show that the main reasons behind a family's school choice is the proximity to the student's home or parents' workplace. In addition, parents do not have the necessary information to compare the quality of schools.

A second questionable characteristic is that public schools are forced to accept all students, whereas private subsidized schools can select students in accordance with their education objectives. Furthermore, private subsidized schools are allowed to operate for profit. As such, to minimize costs, private subsidized schools have incentives to select students that are less expensive to educate: students with better skills and from higher socioeconomic groups. Indeed, if the school's objective is to improve its absolute performance in standardized tests, it could foreseeably be expected to choose better skilled students with higher social capital because this would allow costs to be reduced and competitiveness to be increased (Epple and Romano 1998). It is also argued that these practices would not occur in a competitive environment because private subsidized schools would have incentives to admit all students, since that would be the way to maximize gains. However, the limited evidence found in Chile suggests that choosing students could be a significant phenomenon.[4]

We provide evidence on the use of student selection mechanisms applied by private subsidized schools in a competitive context. We also look at the effect of selection on academic results in standardized tests. The screening criteria are grouped into three categories: student ability, socioeconomic group, and religious selection.[5] The total impact of the screening is captured by the direct selection effect; the indirect effect is measured through the benefit of attending a school in which the socioeconomic profile of students is higher than that of schools without selection.

This study uses individual information from the 2005 SIMCE for fourth grade primary students. The evidence indicates that the different selection methods are widely used by private subsidized schools, and especially in schools with high socioeconomic profiles. As the theory suggests, student ability selection is the most frequently used and produces significant effects on subsequent academic outcomes. The results show that the public-private gap observed in earlier studies disappears after controlling for the selection criteria used.

In summary, we present a new analysis of some features of the education design that alter the incentives schools face, which in turn affect the expected competition in the education market. Because parents choose schools mainly by their proximity to either home or workplace and public schools must receive all students applying, subsidized schools are able to select the best students. Our results show that selection practices are relevant to explain academic performance, while the public-private gap previously reported by other studies disappears. Although we do not have an econometric instrument to identify causality, we argue that because the evidence for Chile shows that results do not drive parents' decisions, it is not likely that schools with higher academic performance attract more students. Therefore, causality is expected to run from selection to results.

This study is structured into four sections. This introductory section is followed by a brief description of the Chilean education system. Section 3 contains a description of the data and the methodology used in the study; in the last part of the section we explain the main findings. The conclusions are presented in the final section.

The Education System in Chile: How Well Is It Working?

The Chilean education system underwent significant modifications in the 1980s as a result of a far-reaching program of reforms implemented by the military government (1973–90). The reforms included decentralizing the administration of education establishments by transferring the administration of public schools from the Ministry of Education to the Municipal Authorities.[6] A nationwide voucher system involving publicly and privately administered schools was also included.[7] The reform introduced a uniform demand-side subsidy in which parents are free to choose among the schools in the market.

As a result, education in Chile shifted to three kinds of administrative alternatives: municipal establishments (PUs) funded by the student subsidy provided by the state and under municipal administration, private subsidized establishments (PSs) funded by the student subsidy and administered by the private sector, and private fee-paying establishments (PPs) funded and administered by the private sector.[8]

Unlike with voucher schemes implemented in other countries, private schools in Chile can choose their students.[9] Municipal schools, however, are prohibited from choosing, except in cases in which the demand for places exceeds the availability. Finally, private subsidized schools can belong to for-profit or not-for-profit organizations.[10]

Numerous studies have analyzed the impact of the voucher program in Chile. Many of them examine the public-private gap in academic results and the effects of competition on it. However, these studies do not take into account the screening practices conducted by schools.

By using the education production function approach, McEwan and Carnoy (1998) studied the effect of competition on the Chilean education system. They used the results of the SIMCE tests from 1988 to 1996. A measure of competition was defined as the percentage of private subsidized school admissions in each municipality. The results of the model with fixed effects per school show a negative effect of competition: municipalities with higher admissions levels in private schools have public schools with lower SIMCE results. The authors argue that the negative relationship between competition and results in public schools is produced by the migration of the best students to private schools (sorting).

Mizala and Romaguera (2000) estimate education production functions using the 1996 SIMCE test data (fourth grade primary school). The SIMCE results of each establishment are regressed against a vector of socioeconomic variables (income brackets, vulnerability index), school variables (teacher experience, teacher/student ratio, number of schools, geographic area), and student characteristics (preschool attendance). The main finding of the article suggests that once the variables described are controlled for, there are small but statistically significant differences in the SIMCE results between public and private subsidized schools.

Gallego (2002) seeks to estimate the effects of competition in the context of the incentives provided by the policy framework and market structure. The article has a theoretical market framework based on the literature on incentives, competition, and information. The empirical work is based on the SIMCE test results for the 1994–97 period. The estimate relates the competition variable, measured as the percentage of private school admissions in the municipality, with establishment-level SIMCE results. The fraction of the urban population and the number of students in the municipality are used as instruments to treat the endogenous condition of the competition variable. These variables are related to the decision of offering education in a municipality, but they are not correlated with education results. Considering the universe of private subsidized schools, the results show that competition contributes to a better establishment-level SIMCE average. The effect of competition increases when only one sample of private subsidized schools is used, suggesting that the incentive structure matters because private schools are more subject to competition.

McEwan (2001, 2003) examines the change in the public-private gap when the socioeconomic level of families and peer effects are included. In addition, the article models parental school choice (municipal versus private subsidized). By taking into account the geographic availability of different types of establishments, it assumes that that variable is correlated to school choice, but not to student ability. Finally, it places special emphasis on the results gaps associated with Catholic schools.

After controlling for selection bias and peer effects, the evidence from the literature for Chile indicates that the gap between public and private subsidized schools is positive and small. However, none of the earlier studies controlled for the selection criteria used by schools.

In general, international academic studies conclude that the students' socioeconomic characteristics are the main determinant of academic achievement. In other words, the wealth of student households leads to better academic results. Given this, in the Chilean case as may be expected, schools use selection practices to obtain the best students to improve their own results.

Epple and Romano (1998) show that schools will choose the highest-ability students from the highest-income families by simulating parental behavior in a free choice system. This is because less capable students imply higher education costs. In other words, less capable students require greater resources than higher-ability students to achieve the same results. Teachers must also spend more time with students with learning difficulties, thus negatively affecting the other students. Therefore, if the objective of private subsidized schools is to maximize gains, then student selection is an easy and economical method for attaining those goals and improving academic results.

Even though the design of the Chilean education system offers the option of choice as a benefit in itself, the evidence suggests that competition tends to favor middle- and high-income families. Hsieh and Urquiola (2006) show that a clear consequence of competition in Chile was to produce a large-scale segmentation of the education system. According to the authors, private subsidized schools did not respond to the competitive pressures of the market model by raising their productivity, but rather by choosing the best students. This may also explain why better results are not observed in public schools.

Adding to the evidence of segregation in Hsieh and Urquiola (2006), this chapter contributes with evidence on the types and uses of school selection methods and their impact on results. This chapter complements Hsieh and Urquiola (2006) by making an in-depth analysis of the mechanisms through which segregation occurs and their effects on academic results.

Data, Methodology, and Results

This chapter uses the database of the standardized SIMCE tests applied to fourth grade primary students in 2005. The test is divided into mathematics, language, and science modules. The SIMCE test is applied to all education establishments of the country. The academic results are complemented by information on the establishments and the socioeconomic characteristics of the families. The latter information is gathered through a questionnaire for parents that includes questions on the student selection criteria used. The sample used includes 161,619 students from municipal and private subsidized establishments from around the country.[11]

The 2005 SIMCE parental questionnaire included questions on the requirements or background information that were requested when the student was admitted. There are three main reasons for student selection. Selection by abilities indicates the cases in which students had to attend a game session or had to do a written or admissions exam. Socioeconomic selection indicates that parents had to present a certificate of income or attend a parental interview at the school. Finally, selection by religious reasons indicates cases in which parents said that the school had requested a baptismal or church marriage certificate.

The methodology used to examine the impact of selection on academic performance follows the production function approach. The dependent variable corresponds to the 2005 mathematics and language SIMCE scores. Two groups of variables are included that explain academic performance: (1) student and household characteristics, including student gender, parental schooling, and household income and size, and (2) establishment and teacher characteristics, such as geographic area, number of students per class, fourth grade primary school admissions size, age, experience, gender, and teacher's postgraduate qualifications.

The main variables of interest for this study are the school's administrative management and the school's student selection criteria. We define a dichotomic variable that takes the value of 1 if the student attended a private subsidized school and 0 if otherwise. Meanwhile, the selection indicators used correspond to ability, socioeconomic status, and selection for religious reasons. A dummy variable is defined for each of these selection criteria, which takes the value of 1 if the school applies selection criteria and 0 if otherwise. Finally, a group of variables was included to capture the characteristics of the students' peers. These used the schooling of the peers' mothers and the peers' fathers and the average household income in the school.

Results

This section examines the effects of schools' student selection on the public-private gap and its impact on the academic performance of students. For this, we first replicate the results of the earlier literature using OLS and IV as estimation methods. The objective is thereby to show that the data and methodology used are neutral with regard to the earlier evidence. In a second stage, the results of the estimates are presented when the student selection criteria are controlled for. Finally, we quantify the effects of selection through their direct effects (selection parameters) and indirect effects (peer effects) based on the results obtained.

The analysis of the 2005 SIMCE data reveals that schools in Chile extensively use selection mechanisms to select the most advantaged students, including admissions tests, parental interviews, and minimum scores. This study identifies three criteria for measuring selection: child's ability, socioeconomic group, and religion.

The data indicate that more than 31 percent of students underwent some selection process when they were admitted into their present schools at the time of the SIMCE test. This proportion practically doubles in the case of private subsidized schools. Only 1 percent of all students underwent all the selection criteria.

With regard to student selection by private subsidized schools, 48 percent of students were chosen by ability, 26 percent by socioeconomic status, and 20 percent by religion or values. In contrast, municipal schools hardly ever use selection.

We also observed a pattern of increasing selection as socioeconomic level rises, which also applies to private subsidized and municipal schools. For instance, on average, 66 percent of students from the highest decile were chosen by some of the screening criteria. As expected, although the trend is similar, the degree of selection varies significantly among types of schools.

Thus, the evidence on the selection strategy used by Chilean private subsidized schools is consistent with the theory. The selection processes students face vary depending on their socioeconomic level and the type of schools to which they apply (private or municipal).

Private subsidized schools commonly use selection mechanisms, with student ability and family income as the most recurrent. Schools that use selection can be expected to reduce their education costs through these mechanisms and also to achieve better results than schools that do not.

Replicating Earlier Results: Public-Private Gap

As previously mentioned, the first studies that sought to quantify the public-private education gap in Chile used SIMCE data and OLS as estimation methods. After controlling for the socioeconomic characteristics of the student and the establishment characteristics, the results indicate that a child who attends a private subsidized school obtains 9.5 additional points in mathematics than a child in a municipal school. This result replicates earlier studies.[12]

In addition to the controls above, we added peer effects on results as an additional explanatory variable. This peer control includes the average schooling of classmates' fathers and mothers and classmates' household income. In this case, the gap favoring private subsidized schools drops to 2.5 points, which is also consistent with results from the previous literature.

As discussed earlier, the results above could have selection bias as a result of the choice of school type by parents. Therefore, other studies have estimated school choice in a first stage, using the supply of municipal and private subsidized establishments at a municipal level as an instrumental variable.

Results indicate that the higher the schooling level of the parents, the higher is the probability of attending private subsidized schools. This positive relationship is also observed between income and the above probability. In other words, parents with more resources have a higher probability of sending their children to those kinds of schools. In addition, the instruments show that the higher the degree of availability of municipal schools, the lower is the probability of attending private subsidized schools. In contrast, the greater the degree of availability of private subsidized schools, the higher is the likelihood of attending those schools.

The results of earlier studies are replicated under IV methodology. These estimates show that after controlling for peer effects, the gap favoring private subsidized schools is positive and small.

In summary, the data and methodology used in this study replicate the results reported in the literature, without controlling for the different selection categories. As such, after controlling for student selection, it can be indicated that the results of the estimates presented below are independent of the data and the methodology used.

A first result of interest is measuring the effect on the public-private gap of including these additional controls. The estimates indicate that after controlling for the school, household, peer, and individual characteristics, the impact of attending a private subsidized school declines as the selection criteria are controlled for. In fact, the contribution of attending private subsidized schools is 2.5 additional points on average, without controlling for student selection criteria.

However, after controlling for school, individual, and household characteristics, the parameters associated with the various types of selection are positive and statistically significant in all estimates. These results suggest that students who underwent some selection process obtained better results than those who did not.

After controlling for the three selection criteria simultaneously, the evidence shows that selection by ability has the greatest impact on academic performance, with more than 6.6 additional points over the sample average. The impact of selection by abilities represents 13 percent of the standard unconditional deviation of the mathematics SIMCE scores. Selection by socioeconomic level has the lowest impact, barely representing more than 1 additional point. Selection for religious reasons has the second highest impact, contributing more than 2 additional points.[13]

Therefore, if a school uses the three selection methods discussed above, its students obtain 10 additional points on average compared with students from schools with no selection. This is almost 20 percent of the standard unconditional deviation of the mathematics SIMCE scores.[14]

After controlling for all the selection criteria, the parameter associated with the public-private gap remains positive but not statistically significant. These results indicate that the positive, small, and statistically significant gap reported in earlier studies is explained by the selection criteria of private subsidized schools, rather than by education advantages of those schools.

Finally, it is to be expected that student selection practices based on shared criteria in the school will have an impact on the heterogeneity of the results in the school. Indeed, students in a given school would be more homogenous after a selection process. It could also therefore be expected that the variance of results in schools that use selection will be lower than that in schools that do not. Estimates in cases in which the dependent variable corresponds to the intraschool standard deviation of the results in the SIMCE test indicate that private subsidized schools have a lower dispersion of results than municipal schools. In addition, the results indicate that the dispersion of the SIMCE scores drops when selection by abilities and socioeconomic status is used, selection on religious grounds having the most significance. The effects of income and socioeconomic selection on dispersion in the language test are statistically significant.

Proving Robustness: Estimates by Instrumental Variables

As discussed earlier, results on the public-private gap could be explained by the endogeneity of school choice by parents. We examine whether the results of modeling school choice affect the results of the student selection process. For this, the type of school is modeled using the education supply in the municipality of residence of the student's family as an instrument.

Meanwhile, a second source of selection could be self-selection by parents who choose schools based on their quality. This could potentially produce a problem of simultaneity between the selection made by parents and by schools, which could bias the estimated parameters. However, according to Elacqua, Schneider, and Buckley (2006) the main reasons explaining the families' choice of schools are related to their nearness to home or workplace. In addition, parents do not have the necessary information to distinguish the quality of schools. So, the screening to be examined is that done by schools.

The results show that the impact of selection on education performance is robust when considering the type of school chosen by families in a first stage.

Concerning the public-private gap, it should be highlighted that the results of the estimates by IV, after correcting for the problems of endogeneity, show that the gap favoring private subsidized schools drops to zero in statistical terms.

In summary, the estimates by OLS and IV indicate that, after controlling for family and school characteristics and student selection criteria, the public-private gap is statistically equal to zero. These estimates suggest that the selection criteria used by private subsidized schools are relevant variables for explaining the higher SIMCE test scores that they obtain relative to municipal schools.

Quantifying the Effects: Direct and Indirect Effects of Student Selection

As has already been explained, schools that use screening criteria choose students with the best characteristics, who are consequently cheaper to educate. We will call this the direct effect of student selection. However, the use of selection mechanisms has a second effect in regard to academic performance. In fact, the selection process also improves the characteristics of the peers. We will call this the indirect effect. It is important to note that the earlier specifications control for peer effects. However, the effect indicated here differs from the peer effect because it considers the benefits associated with peer selection more than their direct contribution.

The results indicate that a student who attends a school that selects by ability obtains (simply by having passed those selection criteria) a score 2.8 percent above students who attend a school without selection. The indirect effect of attending a school with a better level of peers adds 4.6 percent in the case of selection by abilities. As such, a student who attends a school that selects by abilities obtains a SIMCE score in mathematics 7.4 percent above that of a student in a school that does not select. As may be expected, the best results are obtained by students who attend schools that use all the selection methods. These students obtain a total score 13.6 percent higher than students from schools that do not select.

Conclusion

The provision of education through the introduction of competition and incentive mechanisms (demand-side subsidies or vouchers) has been widely debated in the literature. This kind of system was implemented in Chile in the early 1980s; it is one of the few nationwide systems in the world and is backed by more than 20 years of data. This scheme contemplates a direct common subsidy to education establishments from the government for each student admitted to a public or private subsidized school.

The framework assumes the existence of an education market that operates as expected. There are at least two characteristics of the Chilean system that call into question the functionality of this market. First, the evidence suggests that parents do not necessarily choose schools on the basis of quality, which is a key element for strengthening (weakening) good (bad) schools. In fact, Elacqua, Schneider, and Buckley (2006) show that the main reasons behind a family's school choice is the nearness to home or workplace.

A second questionable characteristic is that public schools are obligated to accept all students, whereas private subsidized schools can select students in accordance with their education objectives. Furthermore, private subsidized schools are allowed to operate for profit. As such, to minimize costs, private subsidized schools will logically select students that are less expensive to educate. The process of selection also improves the peer average characteristics (indirect effect).

This study provides evidence on the use of student selection mechanisms in Chile applied by private subsidized schools in a competitive context. As the theory suggests, student ability selection is the most frequently used and produces the greatest effects on subsequent academic results. The results by OLS and IV indicate that, after controlling for family and school characteristics and student selection criteria, the public-private gap shown in earlier studies drops to zero. Because parents reveal that they do not choose schools by academic quality, causality is likely to run from selection to results, not the other way around.

In summary, holding all else constant, a student attending a school that uses selection criteria obtains results in standardized mathematics tests 7 percent to 10 percent higher than a student from a school that does not use selection. This evidence should not be considered to prove the failure of the voucher system but as elements to take into account to improve its design and functionality.

Further research should be conducted to understand why some schools have excess demand and how this market reacts to the existence of rents that could be appropriated by entrance of new establishments.

Notes

1. See Arrow, Bowles, and Durlauf (2000) for a range of interdisciplinary articles that highlight the importance of education in reducing income inequality and fostering social mobility.

2. Hanushek (1986), Hanushek (1996), and Hanushek, Rivkin, and Taylor (1996) have demonstrated this by using sample information for various countries.

3. For an analysis and discussion of the Chilean education model, see McEwan (2001); McEwan (2003); Hsieh and Urquiola (2006); and Gauri (1999).

4. Parry (1996) provides preliminary evidence on the selection practices used in Chilean schools concerning admission exams, minimum grades, behavior reports, and parental interviews. The study includes an exercise similar to the one proposed here, but its results and interpretation are limited because the data are based on a small sample chosen by the author (only 48 observations). Information on the various selection practices comes from interviews with school principals, which could bias the extent of the results. Our study uses a large sample with information provided by parents.

5. These selection categories come from questions to parents in the 2005 SIMCE fourth grade test .

6. That is why these kinds of establishments became known as municipal schools. The reform also implied termination of the contracts between the Ministry of Education and the teachers, forcing the teachers to choose between becoming municipal employees or quitting and joining the private sector.

7. As indicated by Gauri (1999), the political circumstances under which the voucher system was established are determinant in its implementation. Establishing such a system under a democratic government could have required long and profound discussions and empirical evidence of its expected benefits.

8. Before the reform, there were already private subsidized schools, belonging mainly to nonprofit religious institutions, with subsidies that were 50 percent of those given to public schools. For a more detailed description of the Chilean education system, see the works of Gauri (1999) and Tessada (1998).

9. For example, in the Netherlands and Belgium the private sector plays a significant role in education. However, those schools do not select students.

10. Although in 1981 most private subsidized schools belonged to religious institutions, after the reform most of the new schools were for-profit. For example, 84 percent of new schools in 1988 belonged to for-profit institutions (Hsieh and Urquiola 2006).

11. This study, like most of the previous literature for Chile, included only private subsidized and municipal schools mainly because private fee-paying schools (8 percent of the total students), which do not receive public funding, constitute a completely different market.

12. See Bravo, Contreras, and Sanhueza (1999) and Mizala and Romaguera (2000).

13. We also have some estimates, available on request, using the fee charged to parents as indicated by their answers in the SIMCE questionnaire. We did not use this variable in our main estimations for two reasons: not all parents answered this question and there is a great deal of variance within schools. Nevertheless, even when controlling by fees, the results do not change.

14. Even though this result is significant, only 1 percent of students are selected with all four criteria.

References

Arrow, K., S. Bowles, and S. Durlauf (eds.). 2000. *Meritocracy and Economic Inequality.* Princeton, NJ: Princeton University Press.

Bravo, D., D. Contreras, and C. Sanhueza. 1999. "Educational Achievement, Inequalities and Private-Public Gap: Chile 1982–1997." Working paper. Department of Economics, University of Chile.

Elacqua, G., M. Schneider, and J. Buckley. 2006. "School Choice in Chile: Is It Class or the Classroom?" *Journal of Policy Analysis and Management* 25: 577–601.

Epple, D., and R. Romano. 1998. "Competition between Private and Public Schools, Vouchers and Peer Group Effects." *American Economic Review* 62 (1): 33–62.

Gallego, F. 2002. "Competencia y resultados educativos: teoria y evidencia para chile." *Cuadernos de Economía* 39: 309–52.

Gauri, V. 1999. *School Choice in Chile: Two Decades of Educational Reform.* Pittsburgh, PA: University of Pittsburgh Press.

Hanushek, E. A. 1986. "The Economics of Schooling: Production and Efficiency in Public Schools." *Journal of Economic Literature* 24: 1141–77.

———. 1996. "A More Complete Picture of School Resource Policies." *Review of Educational Research* 66: 397–409.

Hanushek, E. A., S. G. Rivkin, and L. L. Taylor. 1996. "Aggregation and the Estimated Effects of School Resources." *The Review of Economics and Statistics* 78: 611–27.

Hsieh, C.-T., and M. Urquiola. 2006, "The Effects of Generalized School Choice on Achievement and Stratification: Evidence from Chile's Voucher Program." *Journal of Public Economics* 90: 1477–1503.

McEwan, P. 2003. "Peer Effects on Student Achievement: Evidence from Chile." *Economics of Education Review* 22: 131–41.

McEwan, P. J. 2001. "The Effectiveness of Public, Catholic, and Non-religious Private Schools in Chile's Voucher System." *Education Economics* 9: 103–128.

McEwan, P. J. and M. Carnoy. 1998. Choice between Private and Public Schools in a Voucher System: Evidence from Chile. Mimeo. Stanford University.

Mizala, A., and P. Romaguera. 2000. "School Performance and Choice: The Chilean Experience." *Journal of Human Resources* 35: 392–417.

Parry, T. R. 1996. "Will Pursuit of Higher Quality Sacrifice Equal Opportunity in Education? An Analysis of the Education Voucher System in Santiago." *Social Science Quarterly* 77: 821–41.

Tessada, J. 1998. "La educación en chile: Nuevas reformas y revisión de la situación nuevas reformas y revisión de la situación actual." Seminario de título Instituto de Economía, PUC (Pontificia Universidad Católica).

CHAPTER 5

Education Vouchers in Colombia

Eric Bettinger, Michael Kremer, and Juan E. Saavedra

Introduction

The view that private schools function better than public schools in the developing world has prompted calls for governments in poor countries to experiment with demand-side financing programs such as vouchers (Psacharopolous et al. 1986). This chapter presents evidence on the impact of a voucher program implemented in 1991 in Colombia. Specifically, the analysis is centered on the mechanism by which the program increased learning outcomes.

The Colombian government established the Programa de Ampliación de Cobertura de la Educación Secundaria (PACES), or Program for Coverage Expansion in Secondary Education, in late 1991 in an attempt to expand private provision of public services (King et al. 1997). The program, which was funded partly by the World Bank, also aimed to increase secondary school enrollment rates (King et al. 1998). Figures from 1993 show that only 78 percent of age-eligible children in Colombia and only 55 percent of children from the poorest quintile of the population were enrolled in secondary school (Sánchez and Núñez 1995).

Since it was inaugurated in 1991, PACES has provided more than 125,000 pupils with vouchers covering somewhat more than half the average cost of private secondary school. The PACES program operated in all large cities in the country and targeted low-income families by offering vouchers to children living in neighborhoods classified into the two lowest socioeconomic strata (of six) who attended public primary schools.[1] The families could use the vouchers to pay for their children to attend any participating private school.

Families had to submit a utility bill to establish their place of residence and, thus, their eligibility for the voucher scheme.[2] To qualify for a voucher, applicants had to be entering the Colombian secondary school cycle, which begins with grade 6, and be 15 years of age or younger. Before applying, the students must already have been admitted to a participating secondary school (in other words, one that would accept the voucher).

The maximum value of the voucher (US$190) was initially set at a level equivalent to the average tuition fee in low- to middle-cost private schools in Colombia's three largest cities. Schools charging less than the vouchers' face value received only their usual tuition. Matriculation and monthly fees for private schools attended by voucher applicants in 1998 averaged about $340, so most voucher recipients had to supplement the voucher with private funds to meet the tuition costs.

Participating private schools included for-profit schools, religious-affiliated schools, and schools run by charitable foundations. Initially, vouchers could be used at for-profit and nonprofit schools, but after 1996, for-profit schools were excluded. Participating schools had to be located in participating towns, which included all Colombia's largest cities. Just under half of private schools in the 10 largest cities accepted vouchers in 1993. Participating schools tended to serve lower-income pupils and to have lower tuition than nonparticipating private schools. Schools with a vocational curriculum were also overrepresented among those in the program.

Test score comparisons reported by King et al. (1997) showed that achievement levels in participating private schools were very close to those in public schools, although they were still significantly below achievement levels in nonparticipating private schools. Pupil-teacher ratios and facilities were similar in public and participating private schools, but nonparticipating private schools had lower pupil-teacher ratios and better facilities. Relatively elite private schools opted out of the PACES program, probably because of delays in paying the voucher funds to schools on the part of the Colombian Institute for Education, Credit, and Training Abroad, which ran the program. Moreover, some school managers may have viewed the prospect of an influx of pupils from low-income backgrounds as undesirable. However, many private schools in Colombia that served low-income populations apparently welcomed the PACES program.

Voucher recipients were eligible for automatic renewal through 11th grade (when Colombian high school ends) provided that the recipients' academic performance warranted their promotion to the next grade. Students who failed a grade were supposed to be dropped from the PACES program. Figures in Calderón (1996) showed that, on average, 77 percent of recipients renewed their vouchers. By way of comparison, the national high school promotion rate was about 70 percent.

When demand for these vouchers exceeded supply, most cities and towns used lotteries to allocate them. Municipal governments paid 20 percent of the cost of the vouchers, and the central government paid 80 percent. Each municipality decided how many vouchers to fund, subject to a maximum allocated to towns by the central government. This allocation was determined by estimating the shortfall between primary school enrollment and the available space in public secondary schools. As a result, voucher award rates varied considerably by city and year depending on the ratio of applicants to available vouchers.

Evidence from a Randomized Natural Experiment

Because in many cities the PACES vouchers were awarded by lottery, the first assessment of PACES used a quasi-experimental research design comparing the education and other outcomes of lottery winners and losers (Angrist et al. 2002, 2006). Subject to a variety of caveats, this methodology provided evidence of program effects similar to what would have been yielded by a randomized trial. The authors used a simple regression model (based on the lottery) and two-stage least squares, using the lottery as the instrument.

Beginning in the summer of 1998, telephone interviews were conducted with roughly 1,600 PACES applicants from the 1995 and 1997 cohorts from Bogotá and the 1993 applicant cohort from Jamundí, a suburb of Cali, stratifying the sample to obtain approximately equal numbers of winners and losers. This constituted about 55 percent of lottery winners and 53 percent of lottery losers. Because the response probability was virtually uncorrelated with voucher status, little bias is likely to have been introduced from the fact that not all applicants were interviewed.

The authors found that there were no significant differences between lottery winners and losers in enrollment three years after application, with most pupils in both the winner and loser groups still being enrolled in secondary school. However, lottery winners were 15 percentage points more likely to be attending private schools than public schools, had completed an additional 0.1 years of school, and were about 10 percentage points more likely than losers to have completed eighth grade.[3] Although high rates of grade repetition are a widely recognized problem in Latin America (see Jacoby 1994; Psacharopoulos and Veléz 1993), reduced repetition does not necessarily mean higher learning. Therefore, the authors administered achievement tests to a subset of the pupils surveyed. The test results suggested that, on average, lottery winners scored about 0.2 standard deviations higher than losers, a large but only marginally significant difference. The effect on girls was larger and more precisely estimated than the effect on boys.

In addition to increased education attainment and academic achievement, lottery winners were less likely than losers to be married or cohabiting, and they worked about 1.2 fewer hours per week (again, this difference was found mostly for girls). Both of these results suggest that lottery winners had a greater focus on schooling than the losers.

The program clearly shifted some participants from public to private school, and pupils who shifted may have benefited from the opportunity to attend private schools. There is also evidence that some pupils who would have attended private school anyway were able to attend more expensive private schools. Finally, voucher recipients may have had a greater incentive to focus on their schooling because their vouchers were renewed only if they graduated to the next grade.

Evidence from Administrative Records

Previous research on primary and secondary school vouchers has tended to focus on the short-term effects that vouchers have on test scores. Missing from most of these studies has been an assessment of how vouchers affect longer-term outcomes, such as high school graduation rates, which are more clearly tied to students' eventual economic success.

Therefore, a second assessment of Colombia's PACES program examined its longer-term effects by looking at the impact of winning the voucher lottery on students' outcomes seven years after the fact. The authors used administrative data from Colombia's centralized college entrance examinations, the ICFES, to estimate how the receipt of vouchers affected high school graduation rates and academic achievement. ICFES registration is a good proxy for high school graduation, because 90 percent of all graduating high school seniors take the exam (World Bank

1993). Using administrative records allows the estimation of long-term effects, and also these data are much less expensive to obtain than survey data and scores from a specialized testing program.

The sample yielded by these administrative data was limited to Bogotá, for 1999 and 2001, seven and nine years after the program was inaugurated. Because in many places PACES vouchers were awarded by lottery, this random assignment of vouchers made it possible to use a natural experiment research design in which losers provided a comparison group for winners. For the estimation, the authors used regression analysis between winners and losers. Because proportionally more lottery winners than losers took the ICFES exam, any direct comparison of test scores for winners and losers would be subject to selection bias. Therefore, the authors used parametric estimation and nonparametric quantile-specific bounds estimation to counter this selection bias.

The assessment found that, after an adjustment for selection bias, voucher winners had substantially higher high school graduation rates and test scores than losers. The fact that lottery winners were substantially more likely than losers to score in the top quartile of the national university entrance exam suggests that the PACES program increased learning not only by increasing incentives for students to avoid repeating grades but also in other ways such as by increasing school choice.

School(s) Survey

Most voucher studies measure only the impact of vouchers on student achievement but not their impact on others (Bettinger et al. 2004). One theory that has been put forward is that, although vouchers may benefit students by moving them to schools with higher-achieving peers, vouchers may not increase average education achievement in society (see, for example, Epple and Romano 1998; Hsieh and Urquiola 2006). According to this theory, vouchers have positive effects for participants because voucher recipients move to schools in which their peers have better academic records than those in the recipients' former schools. However, the movement of voucher students from traditional public schools to private schools may actually have had a negative impact on their new peers and perhaps on those left behind in the public schools.

One way to disentangle hypotheses about the impact of peer effects is to identify a population of voucher winners who do not move to schools with superior characteristics (such as higher academic achievement) and measure the effect of vouchers in this specific group. This was the approach taken in a third assessment of Colombia's voucher program, which identified a set of voucher winners who did not move to schools with peers with superior observable characteristics—those who applied to private vocational schools.

In the Colombian voucher program, students had to apply and be accepted at a private school before they could apply for the voucher. Students could apply to either academic or vocational private schools (*escuelas técnicas*). In general, academic schools are more prestigious than vocational schools and have students who are more likely to complete secondary school and to obtain high exam scores. Once the students had applied, a lottery was used to determine which students received the voucher. Voucher winners tended to stay in the same school once accepted because it was administratively difficult to retain the voucher if they switched schools. Fewer than 20 percent of students who transferred after the first year of the voucher were able to retain their vouchers.

The authors of this study used three sources of information to compare outcomes in vocational schools with those in academic schools in the city of Bogotá—the phone interviews that had been conducted for the first study, administrative data from the ICFES, and a survey of a sample of vocational and academic schools in Bogotá. The results were then estimated using regression analysis controlling for peer effects.

Among applicants to vocational private schools, the authors found that voucher lottery winners were more likely to stay in vocational schools, whereas lottery losers were more likely to change to an academic school. They also found that, among applicants to vocational schools, voucher lottery winners attended schools with higher dropout rates, fewer qualified teachers, and lower fees than academic schools. Despite this, the authors found that lottery winners in this population had better education outcomes than losers in the better schools, including higher graduation rates and reading test scores. They were also more likely to stay in private school, more likely to finish eighth grade, and less likely to repeat a grade. Furthermore, they were more likely to take the college entrance exam and, if they took the exam, more likely to pass it.

This casts doubt on the argument that voucher effects operate entirely through enabling voucher winners to associate with more high-achieving peers, at least in Colombia.

Conclusion

On balance, the results of these three assessments of PACES in Colombia suggest that there has been a substantial gain in high school graduation rates and achievement as a result of the voucher program. Although the benefits of achievement gains per se are hard to quantify, there is a substantial economic return to high school graduation in Colombia. At a minimum, this suggests that demand-side financing efforts similar to the PACES program warrant further study.

An unresolved question, however, is how to reconcile the consistently positive voucher effects for Colombia reported here with more mixed results for the United States (see, for example, Howell and Peterson 2002; Rouse 1998). One possibility is that PACES is a better experiment and included features not necessarily shared by other voucher programs, such as incentives for academic advancement and the opportunity for those who would have gone to private school anyway to use vouchers to attend more expensive schools. Another possible explanation for divergent effects is a larger gap in the quality of public and private schools in Colombia than in the United States.

Notes

1. Almost half of all children from the richest income quintile attended private primary schools.
2. All utility bills in Colombia contain information about the socioeconomic stratum.
3. Primarily because they repeated fewer grades.

References

Angrist, J., E. Bettinger, E. Bloom, E. King, and M. Kremer. 2002. "Vouchers for Private Schooling in Colombia: Evidence from a Randomized Natural Experiment." *The American Economic Review* 92 (5): 1535–58.

Angrist, J., E. Bettinger, and M. Kremer. 2006. "Long-Term Educational Consequences of Secondary School Vouchers: Evidence from Administrative Records in Colombia." *American Economic Review* 96(3): 847–62.

Bettinger, E., M. Kremer, and J. Saavedra. 2004 "How Do Vouchers Work? Evidence from Colombia." Mimeo. Case Western Reserve.

Calderón, A. 1996. "Voucher Programs for Secondary Schools: The Colombian Experience." World Bank Human Capital Development Working Paper No. 66. The World Bank, Washington, DC. http://www.worldbank.org/education/economicsed/finance/demand/related/wp~00066.html.

Epple, D., and R. E. Romano. 1998. "Competition between Private and Public Schools, Vouchers, and Peer-Group Effects" *The American Economic Review* 88 (1): 33–62.

Howell, W. G., and P. E. Peterson. 2002. *The Education Gap: Vouchers and Urban Schools*. Washington, DC: The Brookings Institution Press.

Hsieh, C.-T., and M. Urquiola. 2006. "The Effects of Generalized School Choice on Achievement and Stratification: Evidence from Chile's Voucher Program." *Journal of Public Economics* 90 (8–9): 1477–1503.

Jacoby, H. 1994. "Borrowing Constraints and Progress through School: Evidence from Peru." *Review of Economics and Statistics* 76 (1): 151–60.

King, E., P. Orazem, and D. Wolgemuth. 1998. "Central Mandates and Local Incentives: The Colombia Education Voucher Program." Working Paper No. 6, Series on Impact Evaluation of Education Reforms. Development Economics Research Group, World Bank, Washington, DC, February.

King, E., L. Rawlings, M. Gutierrez, C. Pardo, and C. Torres. 1997. "Colombia's Targeted Education Voucher Program: Features, Coverage and Participation." Working Paper No. 3, Series on Impact Evaluation of Education Reforms. Development Economics Research Group, World Bank, Washington, DC, September.

Psacharopolous, G., and E. Velez. 1993. "Educational Quality and Labor Market Outcomes: Evidence from Bogotá, Colombia." *Sociology of Education* 66 (2): 130–45.

Psacharopolous, G., J. Tan, and E. Jimenez. 1986. *Financing Education in Developing Countries: An Exploration of Policy Options*. Washington, DC: World Bank.

Rouse, C. E. 1998. "Private School Vouchers and Student Achievement: An Evaluation of the Milwaukee Parental Choice Program." *Quarterly Journal of Economics* 113 (2): 553–602.

Sánchez, F., and J. Núñez. 1995. "Por Qué los Niños Pobres No Van a la Escuela? (Determinantes de la asistencia escolar en Colombia)" Mimeo. Departamento Nacional de Planeación, República de Colombia.

World Bank. 1993. *Staff Appraisal Report: Colombia, Secondary Education Project*. Report No. 1 1834-CO. Human Resources Operations Division, Latin America and the Caribbean Region, November 19.

PART II

Faith-Based Providers

CHAPTER 6

The Performance of Decentralized School Systems: Evidence from Fe Y Alegría in República Bolivariana de Venezuela

Hunt Allcott and Daniel E. Ortega

Introduction

Public education in R. B. de Venezuela has deteriorated steadily during the past 25 years. Although the average education attainment of the labor force increased from 6.1 years to 8.2 years and the literacy rate for people 15 and older went from 85 percent to 93 percent between 1981 and 2001, the government's expenditures on education dropped 36 percent in real terms between 1980 and 2003. Average aptitude test scores for high school seniors dropped from 21 to 6 in verbal and from 11 to 3 in math between 1987 and 2003. As a result of the deterioration in the quality of education and changes in the labor market, the Mincerian returns to education have dropped from 15 percent in 1975 to under 10 percent in 2003.

The authors would like to thank Rosa Amelia Gonzalez of the Instituto de Estudios Superiores de Administración (IESA) and administrators at Fe y Alegría, especially Nelbis Aguilar, for their invaluable support during this project. We also appreciate comments from seminar participants at the Latin American and Caribbean Economic Association (LACEA), Network on Inequality and Poverty, and the World Bank. Hunt Allcott acknowledges financial support from the Ochoa Brillembourg Fellowship. Any errors, which are due to the fact that neither of the authors attended a Fe y Alegría school, remain our own.

Working amid this disconcerting evidence is Fe y Alegría, a confederation of Jesuit schools targeting disadvantaged youth. The program's first primary school was established in Catia, a disadvantaged area of Caracas, in a home donated by a local bricklayer. Since then, it has expanded to serve 1.2 million students in 15 Latin American countries. The organization has a number of initiatives, including job training, teacher training, adult and radio education, and support for microbusinesses, but the bulk of its efforts are spent in primary and secondary education. Most observers, from community members to academic researchers, consider Fe y Alegría to be quite successful, but no econometrically satisfying program evaluation has been undertaken.

Through an econometric estimation of average treatment effect (ATE),[1] we compare Fe y Alegría graduates to a control group of Venezuelan public school students using the results of the Prueba de Aptitud Académica (PAA), a math and verbal test similar to the American SAT. Our results, which are consistent across different estimation methods, show that Fe y Alegría students perform slightly—but significantly in a statistical sense—better on both parts of the PAA. We conclude that this effect is due to the institution's organizational behavior: Fe y Alegría does not spend more money per pupil, but it does evidently have different management and cultural characteristics. Specifically, Fe y Alegría's management structure is much more decentralized, giving school principals budgetary authority and the ability to hire and fire teachers. Partially as a result of this decision-making process, the organization has succeeded in instilling a "family feeling" in teachers, staff, and students, which we believe contributes to the treatment effect.

Because Fe y Alegría is both private and decentralized, this research is related to the literature on decentralization of public services and the literature on school privatization. Fe y Alegría represents a scalable alternative to these policy options, as evidenced by its rapid expansion within R. B. de Venezuela and to other countries in the region. As we show, Fe y Alegría merits imitation and greater scale.

Related Literature

Although we do not focus directly on the issue of decentralization of public services, this chapter is related to that literature insofar as it touches on the benefits and pitfalls of having decision rights closer to the individual. Galiani, Gertler, and Schargrodsky (2005) argue that decentralization of public schooling in Argentina in the early 1990s helped improve the quality of education, as measured by standardized test scores, in well-off regions, but had a negative effect in regions that were disadvantaged to begin with. Pães de Barros and Mendonça (1998) suggest that neither school financial autonomy nor local school boards in Brazil play a significant role in primary school performance, but that the principal's appointment power does have a positive and significant effect. Eskeland and Filmer (2002) find a positive correlation between performance and the autonomy of primary schools in Argentina, and King and Ozler (2000) also suggest a positive effect of decentralization on parent participation in school decision making in Nicaragua. Aedo (1998) presents evidence that Chilean schools that have significant decision rights also perform better than centralized schools. More recently, Sawada and Ragatz (2005), di Gropello and Marshall (2005), and Parker (2005), as part of a larger investigation on teacher incentives in Latin America (Vegas 2005), documented education reforms in El Salvador, Honduras, and Nicaragua, respectively, where either through spontaneous community organization or the government's initiative, some autonomy was transferred to local schools. The reported results are mixed, in part because central authorities still retained significant decision-making rights, although key indicators such as teacher absenteeism and the number of teacher strikes did seem to improve as a result of the reforms.

Other alternative school systems have been extensively studied. Private versus public schooling in general has been one topic of interest in both the United States (see, for example, Hanushek 1994; Hoenack 1994; Manski 1992, among others) and developing countries. Private school performance has been compared with that of public schools and has generally been shown to outperform the public system according to several measures. Cox and Jimenez (1990), after controlling for selection issues, show that private schools perform better on standardized tests than public schools in Colombia and in Tanzania, Saavedra (1996) estimates a differential effect of private versus public schooling on the wages of Peruvian workers, and Contreras (2002) estimates a positive effect of the voucher system relative to public schools on test scores in Chile. Also related is the more narrow focus on Catholic schools, which has been undertaken using mostly data for the United States; in particular, Evans and Schwab (1995) show that being Catholic per se does not affect education outcomes, and then use Catholicism as an instrument for student participation in Catholic schools. They use the binary outcome of high school completion, claiming that it is a much more important predictor of future outcomes, and show that Catholic schools outperform public schools.

There is a basic agency problem in the provision of public schooling. The principals (society and parents) contract implicitly with centralized government administrators to provide quality education. The school administrators may have different incentives, and the effects of their actions on school quality are difficult to observe. By making the agents informationally closer to the parents, decentralization and privatization might help to ameliorate the information problem. Empirically, these effects are difficult to tease out because both privatization and decentralization are bundles of policies that combine solutions to some incentive problems but at the same time may cause several others. It is not easy to find instances in which policies are undertaken in a way that allows identification of the impact of each of its components, that is, to disentangle the effect of increased school principal authority from decreased central curriculum design. The articles in Savedoff (1998), although hampered by the natural limitations in the data, provide suggestive evidence as to the importance of these agency problems that may be resolved by means other than decentralization or privatization.

Despite the high regard for Fe y Alegría and the availability of extensive data, no econometric evaluation has been done of the system's effectiveness. Navarro and de la Cruz (1998) evaluate test scores and use student-level demographic controls, but their analysis is restricted to two Fe y Alegría schools in one Venezuelan state. Our analysis also does not provide direct evidence as to the importance of decentralization, but suggests based on anecdotal evidence that this factor plays an important role in explaining the relative success of the Fe y Alegría system. This chapter thus contributes to the discussion on decentralization and private schooling as ways of addressing incentive problems that arise in public administration.

Data

In R. B. de Venezuela, every graduating high school student takes the Prueba de Aptitud Académica, which is in essence the Venezuelan SAT. Extensive background data on each student are also gathered, ranging from the basics of age and gender to the profession of the father and what transportation the student uses to go to school.

In total, there are 413,607 observations of graduating Venezuelan high school students who took the test in 2003. We include only students who are between the ages of 14 and 22, are not night-school students, and actually graduated that year instead of earlier. We then drop the 4,662 students from public schools that are not included in a separate school registry that allows us to identify municipalities. Controlling for other observable variables, this group scores 0.15 standard deviations lower on the verbal section and statistically the same in math, relative to other public school students. Because there is substantial intrastate variation at the municipality level, however, we chose to omit these observations in order to include municipality dummy variables. Because these 4,662 public school students perform relatively poorly, it is likely (depending on which municipality the schools are actually in) that their omission biases downward the estimated treatment effect of Fe y Alegría.

Our final data set includes 46,460 public school students and 2,237 Fe y Alegría students. Table 6.1 shows the mean of each variable for the treated (Fe y Alegría) and nontreated (public schools) cohorts. Test

Table 6.1   Variable Means for Treated and Nontreated

Variable	Fe y Alegría	Public school
Verbal score	0.09	0.00
Math score	0.20	−0.01
Male dummy	0.47	0.40
Married dummy	0.00	0.00
Age	16.96	16.73
Student works	0.03	0.03
Father's prof: Professor or exec	0.06	0.07
Father's prof: Technician	0.09	0.09
Father's prof: Employee	0.29	0.30
Father's prof: Skilled worker	0.37	0.39
Father's prof: Unskilled worker	0.17	0.14
Mother's ed: University	0.08	0.09
Mother's ed: High school	0.21	0.20
Mother's ed: Some high school	0.27	0.28
Mother's ed: Primary	0.39	0.37
Mother's ed: Illiterate	0.04	0.04
House: Luxurious	0.01	0.01
House: Spacious	0.19	0.20
House: Normal	0.51	0.47
House: Deficient	0.24	0.25
House: Very deficient	0.03	0.03
Highest income bracket	0.01	0.01
2nd-highest income bracket	0.01	0.02
3rd-highest income bracket	0.04	0.05
4th-highest income bracket	0.18	0.19
5th-highest income bracket	0.74	0.70
<3 siblings	0.29	0.26
3 siblings	0.24	0.24

(continued)

Table 6.1   Variable Means for Treated and Nontreated *(Continued)*

Variable	Fe y Alegría	Public school
4 siblings	0.19	0.18
5 siblings	0.12	0.13
6 siblings	0.15	0.17
Pay: Parents	0.90	0.90
Pay: Family	0.00	0.01
Pay: Scholarship	0.01	0.01
Pay: Education credit	0.03	0.03
Pay: Student's work	0.05	0.03
Trans: Own auto	0.35	0.32
Trans: Parents' auto	0.24	0.27
Trans: Friends	0.17	0.19
Trans: School bus	0.10	0.10
Trans: Public transit	0.10	0.08
Social class: Highest	0.01	0.01
Social class: 2nd	0.18	0.17
Social class: 3rd	0.50	0.51
Social class: 4th	0.29	0.28
Social class: Lowest	0.02	0.01
Socioeconomic status (calculated)	0.01	0.00

Source: Authors' estimation.

scores are normalized to mean 0, standard deviation 1. Family income, mother's education, house quality, and social class are reported in five classes, with 1 being the "best." Although we could parameterize these variables, we instead use dummy variables for each bucket to retain the maximum flexibility. As we discuss in the results section, this nonparametric form is important because test scores will be nonlinear—and even nonmonotonic—in some of these variables.

Ideally, our program evaluation would compare students who were either selected into Fe y Alegría randomly or selected purely on observable variables with a control group of students who applied and were not selected, and there would be zero or random attrition through dropouts. Such application records are not available, however, and dropouts during primary and secondary school clearly are not random. Our econometric strategy, discussed in the following section, depends on the assumption that there is no unobservable factor correlated with both graduation from Fe y Alegría and test scores. This is often improbable, but in conversations with Venezuelan researchers and Fe y Alegría staff, we have realized that several factors conspire to form a plausible natural experiment.

The key factor behind the natural experiment is that Fe y Alegría schools are oversubscribed. Applications to Fe y Alegría at the primary and secondary school levels vastly outnumber the available spots: central administrators estimate that admit rates are about 35 percent. Each school then admits the poorest children from local neighborhoods in a nonstandardized process. As a result, conditional on having the motivation to apply for Fe y Alegría, which many students do, the selection of students into schools is on wealth and geographic location. Our observed variables capturing income and house quality proxy very nicely for the wealth aspect of schools' admission decisions. However, if the unobservable characteristics causing a student to apply for Fe y Alegría are not widespread among public school students and are positively correlated with test scores, our estimated treatment effect will be biased upward.

Ideally, we would also observe the second implicit selection factor in admissions, proximity of each student's residence to each school. We argue, however, that any differences are independent or weakly correlated with test scores. As part of the program's mission to serve underprivileged children in poor neighborhoods, Fe y Alegría schools were indeed often placed in the poorest neighborhoods. During the life of the program, however, some of these neighborhoods have changed and experienced relative economic growth. In addition, many of the program's schools were once public schools that were transferred to Fe y Alegría at the community's request, and it is not obvious whether these schools would tend to be in "better" or "worse" neighborhoods. We thus assume that the areas near Fe y Alegría schools are econometrically identical to public school districts within the same municipality. If this assumption fails and Fe y Alegría districts are actually "worse," it will bias our treatment effect downward.

Using factor analysis we generate a variable that summarizes socioeconomic status (see table 6.1). Regressing SES on Fe y Alegría participation and a dummy variable for each municipality indicates that Fe y Alegría students are statistically of the same socioeconomic status as the public school students within their municipality. On the whole, the similarity on observable variables and the reality of the Venezuelan natural experiment suggest that it is reasonable to assume that unobservables do not substantially affect both Fe y Alegría enrollment and test scores.

Econometric Framework

Our fundamental goal will be to calculate the average treatment effect (ATE) typical of the program evaluation literature. The ATE measures the difference between the test score of each unit in both a treated and an untreated state, that is, how a student would have performed in Fe y

Alegría versus how the student would have performed in public school. Given the potential two-way causality between test scores and treatment, we use the instrumental variables method. We had initially planned to use program intensity at the municipal level as an instrument for participation. This identification is comparable with other program evaluation papers such as Duflo's (2001) evaluation of a school construction program or the previous literature on Catholic schools. This strategy requires that the placement of schools not be correlated with unobservables that affect test scores, which we claim above. Unfortunately, there is not enough variation in program intensity at the municipal level to obtain meaningful estimates in the first stage. The highest program intensity is under 25 percent, and even limiting the sample to the 31 municipalities in which there is at least one Fe y Alegría high school, the average is under 5 percent. This makes the estimated ATEs unstable and implausibly high.

After describing above, however, this data set and the natural experiment that created the data lend themselves to estimation of the ATE through ordinary least squares (OLS) and propensity score matching.[2] OLS can provide an estimate of propensity score matching if there is no omitted variables bias. We control for a vector of dummy variables for Venezuelan: male, married, age, student works, father's profession, mother's education, house quality, income, number of siblings, how school fees are paid, transportation to school, and social class.

After calculating the OLS benchmark, we use propensity score matching to estimate the ATE. As discussed in Heckman, Ichimura, and Todd (1997), our data set lends itself to low bias in propensity score matching for two reasons. First, only a few members of the public school control group are outside the range for observed characteristics of the treatment group.[3] Indeed, as the factor analysis and descriptive statistics above show, Fe y Alegría participation appears similar to a natural experiment in that the distributions of many of the observed characteristics are similar, although not statistically identical. Previous studies using propensity score matching with job training programs often struggled with this, specifically that the observed employment rate or wages of the treated were lower than any controls in the pretreatment period. We have eliminated private school students from consideration here precisely because their distribution of observables (and unobservables) is so different in R. B. de Venezuela. Public school students, however, form an excellent control group.

Second, the same questionnaire is administered to both treatment and control, and the two groups are in a "common economic environment."

These issues, of course, relate primarily to problems encountered with evaluation of job training programs. All our data come from the same administration of the same test, with the same demographic questions asked of each student. Furthermore, unlike the case of the American SAT, all graduating Venezuelan high school students take the PAA. Therefore, although the interpretation of the ATE is limited to those students who have not dropped out of school beforehand, there is no selection bias into the test itself.

Although the Fe y Alegría natural experiment described above forms the basis of our assumption of selection on observables, we cannot fully rule out bias due to unobservables. However, the Heckman, Ichimura, and Todd (1997) job training data indicate that this bias is actually less important than the two potential sources of bias above, from which we do not suffer.

The propensity score is the probability that a student with certain observed characteristics will enter Fe y Alegría and graduate from high school versus graduate from a public high school. In the application to school choice, the clear complaint would be that unobservable attributes of students or their families, such as motivation, initiative, or valuation of education, would cause the same types of students who select into Fe y Alegría to also do better in public schools. If these decisions were made in a statistically random way, or through an observable nationally uniform admissions process, this would lend itself to a different estimation strategy. As we discussed in the data section, this is a decentralized admission process that in an unobservable way uses primarily observable variables. As a result, we can consider the propensity score matching results to be unbiased.[4]

Although all graduating students take the test, the ATE is conditional on students actually graduating from high school. Although the range of the observable variables of Fe y Alegría and public school students is effectively the same,[5] there is substantial selection through the years of schooling. Specifically, Fe y Alegría as a policy tries to maintain low dropout rates, and its average promotion rate is 10 percent higher than that in the public sector (González and Arévalo 2005). Thus it is possible that some of the treatment group have unobservables that would have caused them to drop out of public schools; these unobservables would cause the test scores of the treatment group to be lower. This effect will bias the ATE downward.

In our application to Fe y Alegría, while requiring at least some Fe y Alegría students in each municipality, we have observations from municipalities or states in which there are no Fe y Alegría schools, and thus students have effectively zero probability of enrollment in a Fe y Alegría school. If we believed that there were no state- or municipality-level effects on test scores, we would omit the geographic area dummies from the probit estimation, and observations in nonprogram municipalities would have a nonzero propensity score. Because there quite plausibly are geographic-level fixed effects, however, we must include the geographic area dummies. This substantially reduces sample size but still leaves 50,000 observations.

We estimate the probability of being a Fe y Alegría graduate in a traditional fashion, using a probit equation. Heckman, Ichimura, and Todd (1997) and other propensity score matching applications construct higher-order terms and interactions of their observed variables. Because we use only binary variables, we gain nothing from using higher-order terms.

Results

Using the data above and econometric technique, we estimate the ATE in test scores of being a Fe y Alegría student versus being in the public schools. It should be reemphasized that Fe y Alegría is essentially a technical high school, not a college prep, and many of its effects on students are of course not measurable in test scores for college admission.

The OLS results, shown in table A6.1 in the annex, show that Fe y Alegría students perform 0.05 and 0.06 standard deviations higher in verbal score and math score, after correcting for observable characteristics. Especially interesting in these regressions are the coefficients on several of the control variables. As might be expected, younger students tend to do better, as do students with fewer siblings. Instead of linear influences, however, the effects of family income and house quality seem to be in an inverted-U shape. Wealthier students living in "luxurious" houses actually tend to do worse on the exams than poor students. This may be because they have secured university admission through other university-specific tests and thus do not take the PAA as seriously.

Propensity score matching gives similar results. The probit regression used to generate the propensity scores (not shown) confirms anecdotal evidence that well-educated mothers, smaller families, and poorer students tend to be selected for (graduation from) Fe y Alegría. Table 6.2 shows that the ATE for verbal score is 0.1 standard deviations and for math score is 0.08 standard deviations.

Table 6.2   Results of Propensity Score Matching

	Verbal score	Math score
ATE	0.107	0.08
Standard error	0.07	0.03
Obs	46,287	46,287

Source: Authors' estimation.

One potential explanation for the difference between the estimates using OLS and propensity score matching is heterogeneous treatment effects across individuals.[6] If this heterogeneity is present, propensity score matching is the consistent estimator.

Reasons for Fe y Alegría's Improved Performance

We have shown that Fe y Alegría offers a better education than the public schools, as measured by test scores, accounting for population heterogeneity and selection bias. We now suggest potential reasons for the effect. As González and Arévalo (2005) calculate, Fe y Alegría does not spend more money per pupil than public schools. Indeed, teachers do not receive retirement benefits and are thus often forced to view work at Fe y Alegría as a "side job." Thus, differences in financial inputs are not the cause of the improved performance of the program. On the basis of our conversations with school officials and researchers, we suggest key reasons for the program's success.

As a result of its institutional history, Fe y Alegría's structure is different from that of the public schools on several dimensions, as discussed in Navarro and de la Cruz (1998) and González and Arévalo (2005). From the outset, the public school system was not viewed as an effective organizational model, and the initial spirit of volunteerism has morphed into a more established structure. Although religiosity was initially important, individual schools now vary substantially on that measure, with some schools run by nuns and others exhibiting little sign of Catholic influence. The initial growth in the number of schools was financed mainly by local community involvement and private donations, a process that led to significant autonomy at the school level underneath a national umbrella organization led by Father Velaz. This organically developed structure was eventually formally adopted, with the principal and the school council at the center of local decision making and the national leadership dealing with strategic issues such as growth plans and fund raising. Three specific organizational and cultural factors stand out: decentralized decision making, labor flexibility, and the potentially resultant feeling of a "family environment."

School-Level Autonomy. Although there exists a central authority at the national level as in the public system that determines general guidelines and principles for the organization as a whole, each Fe y Alegría school retains substantial administrative autonomy. Each principal can hire and fire teachers, purchase supplies, and sign maintenance contracts, among other things. Each school has the autonomy to plan, budget, procure funding for, and execute infrastructure investments. Although most fund-raising activities for large projects are centrally coordinated, the initiative almost always comes from school-level administrators, whose ideas tend to be encouraged and well received by the national administration. Furthermore, the schools, through the regional offices, play an active role in the national-level budgetary decision making. This contrasts with the public school administration, which is much more highly centralized.

Labor Flexibility. Fe y Alegría teachers are not unionized, and their labor contracts are much more flexible than those of the public school system. Teachers in the public school system are appointed by state-level committees that are often controlled by politically motivated labor unions. In Fe y Alegría, they are hired by the school principal directly and given a one-year trial period before being offered more permanent positions. During this trial period, teachers are not only evaluated on formalities such as meeting the school's schedule of activities (showing up on time to class, grading exams and papers in a timely fashion, attending faculty meetings, etc.), they are monitored in the classroom every quarter and are coached by their more experienced peers. This flexibility relative to the public schools most likely results in a selection process that produces higher teacher quality. Any differences in teacher quality, however, are not the result of higher pay: although its wages for teachers and staff are comparable with outside wages, Fe y Alegría does not offer a retirement plan. As a result, many Fe y Alegría teachers also work in the public schools simply to gain retirement benefits. It seems that Fe y Alegría's compensating differentials are principally the improved teacher training and the esprit de corps.

"Family Feeling." In visits to two Fe y Alegría schools in Catia and to the central administration offices in Caracas, we were struck by what teachers, students, and administrative personnel termed a "family feeling": a sense of belonging to the organization of Fe y Alegría and agreement with the organization's objectives. As described above, this feeling reduces input costs by inducing teachers to work or volunteer longer hours for lower wages. It

also likely increases efficiency of school input use, potentially by inducing students to respect school property more and pay better attention in class. As suggested by the literature in sociological economics such as Akerlof and Kranton (2005), it is possible that Fe y Alegría has succeeded in modifying students' utility functions to value education or discipline more highly. Even without this sort of "indoctrination effect," Fe y Alegría may have simply arrived at a high-performance equilibrium that attracts better teachers and induces continual good performance. Our impression is that this "family feeling" has been instilled in the organization's culture as a matter of policy and is substantially aided by the empowerment associated with school-level autonomy.

Conclusion

Using a large, rich data set, we have shown that graduation from Fe y Alegría increases scores on the Venezuelan college entrance examination relative to counterfactual graduation from public school. The effects are on the order of one-tenth of a standard deviation, statistically significant, and robust to the use of OLS or propensity score matching. Because Fe y Alegría schools are oversubscribed and admit students based on observable poverty and also because the data set is rich and with uniform outcomes, the propensity score matching estimator should be unbiased. These results suggest several further lines of research and policy recommendations.

To strengthen the evaluation of Fe y Alegría, it would certainly be most convincing to randomly select or encourage a cohort to enter the program, creating a true econometric experiment. This would be the most satisfying way to deal with questions about strong ignorability and the exogeneity of participation in the program. In addition, a richer set of outcome variables characterizing the family and economic lives of Fe y Alegría graduates would most likely give a full perspective on the effects of the program. This is not, however, the most interesting line of future research. If we believe that Fe y Alegría offers a better education, it is important to know why, and whether the program can be expanded or whether its successes can be translated to public schools.

If decentralized decision making is indeed a factor in the organization's improved performance, it would suggest that the program of decentralization pursued in Venezuelan schools in the 1990s should be continued more aggressively. On a more basic level, the fact that there is variance in school system quality suggests that policy makers should encourage school variety and choice.

Annex: Regression Results

Table A6.1   OLS Regression Results

Outcome variable:	Verbal score	Math score
Explanatory variables		
Fe y Alegría student	0.05** (0.03)	0.06** (0.01)
Venezuelan citizen	−0.26** (0.01)	−0.4** (0)
Male dummy	0.09** (0)	0.17** (0)
Married dummy	−0.03 (0.77)	−0.18** (0.03)
14 years old	Dropped	Dropped
15 years old	−0.05 (0.59)	−0.11 (0.17)
16 years old	−0.14 (0.11)	−0.21** (0.01)
17 years old	−0.3** (0)	−0.34** (0)
18 years old	−0.46** (0)	−0.47** (0)
19 years old	−0.55** (0)	−0.55** (0)
20 years old	−0.62** (0)	−0.62** (0)
21 years old	−0.6** (0)	−0.54** (0)
22 years old	−0.48** (0)	−0.61** (0)
Student works	−0.06** (0.02)	−0.03 (0.29)
Father's prof: Professor or exec	0.12** (0)	0.1** (0.01)
Father's prof: Technician	0.06 (0.1)	0.03 (0.47)
Father's prof: Employee	0.07** (0.04)	0.07** (0.05)
Father's prof: Skilled worker	0.03 (0.38)	0.02 (0.57)
Father's prof: Unskilled worker	0.04 (0.29)	0.03 (0.39)
Mother's ed: University	0.22** (0)	0.18** (0)
Mother's ed: High school	0.16** (0)	0.13** (0)
Mother's ed: Some high school	0.04 (0.34)	0.06 (0.16)
Mother's ed: Primary	0.04 (0.39)	0.06 (0.16)
Mother's ed: Illiterate	0.05 (0.3)	0.06 (0.19)
House: Luxurious	−0.14** (0.01)	−0.13** (0.02)
House: Spacious	0.14** (0)	0.08** (0.04)
House: Normal	0.22** (0)	0.1** (0.01)
House: Deficient	0.12** (0)	0.05 (0.21)
House: Very deficient	0.06 (0.19)	0.03 (0.52)
Highest income bracket	0.03 (0.57)	−0.05 (0.38)
2nd-highest income bracket	0.06 (0.19)	−0.08* (0.08)
3rd-highest income bracket	0.13** (0)	0.02 (0.61)
4th-highest income bracket	0.21** (0)	0.08** (0.01)
5th-highest income bracket	0.19** (0)	0.06* (0.08)
<3 siblings	0.2** (0)	0.14** (0)
3 siblings	0.15** (0)	0.13** (0)
4 siblings	0.09** (0.04)	0.12** (0)
5 siblings	0.09* (0.06)	0.07* (0.08)
6 siblings	0.03 (0.45)	0.05 (0.27)
Pay: Parents	0.03 (0.43)	0.05 (0.2)

(continued)

Table A6.1   OLS Regression Results

Outcome variable:	Verbal score	Math score
Pay: Family	−0.13* (0.07)	−0.04 (0.53)
Pay: Scholarship	0.07 (0.26)	0.01 (0.87)
Pay: Education credit	0.14** (0.01)	0.11** (0.02)
Pay: Student's work	0.16** (0)	0.15** (0)
Trans: Own auto	−0.06** (0.03)	0 (0.89)
Trans: Parents' auto	0.05** (0.05)	0.09** (0)
Trans: Friends	0.03 (0.21)	0.05** (0.04)
Trans: School bus	0.04 (0.17)	0.05* (0.06)
Trans: Public transit	0.03 (0.31)	0.04 (0.13)
Social class: Highest	−0.07 (0.45)	0.02 (0.79)
Social class: 2nd	−0.32** (0)	−0.15* (0.06)
Social class: 3rd	−0.43** (0)	−0.24** (0)
Social class: 4th	−0.46** (0)	−0.25** (0)
Social class: Lowest	−0.5** (0)	−0.21** (0.02)

Source: Authors' estimations.
* denotes statistical significance at 10%.
** denotes statistical significance at 5%.

Notes

1. The treatment is enrollment in a Fe y Alegría school.
2. Instead of matching (and comparing) observations based on observable characteristics, the propensity score method matches observations based on the probability of participation in the program.
3. This can be rephrased in a more technical way saying that only a few public school students are not on the support of the distribution of the treatment group's observed characteristics.
4. The conditional mean independence assumption is reasonable in this case.
5. We are referring here to the condition of common support.
6. The underlying treatment effects are weighted differently by the two methods: weights applied in matching estimators are proportional to the probability of treatment, whereas the weights applied in OLS are proportional to the variance of treatment (see Angrist 1998).

References

Aedo, C. 1998. "Diferencias entre escuelas y rendimiento estudiantil en Chile" In *La Organización Marca la Diferencia: Educación y Salud en América Latina*, ed. W. Savedoff. Washington, DC: Inter-American Development Bank.

Akerlof, G, and R. Kranton. 2005. "Identity and the Economics of Organizations." *Journal of Economic Perspectives* 19 (1): 9–32.

Angrist, J. 1998. "Estimating the Labor Market Impact of Voluntary Military Service Using Social Security Data on Military Applicants." *Econometrica* 66 (2): 249–88.

Contreras, D. 2002. "Vouchers, School Choice and Access to Higher Education." Mimeo, Universidad de Chile.

Cox, D., and E. Jimenez. 1990. "The Relative Effectiveness of Private and Public Schools: Evidence from two Developing Countries." *Journal of Development Economics* 34 (1–2): 99–121.

di Gropello, E., and J. Marshall. 2005. "Teacher Effort and Schooling Outcomes in Rural Honduras." In *Incentives to Improve Teaching. Lessons from Latin America*, ed. E. Vegas. Washington, DC: World Bank.

Duflo, E. 2001. "Schooling and Labor Market Consequences of School Construction in Indonesia: Evidence from an Unusual Policy Experiment." *American Economic Review* 91 (4): 795–813.

Eskeland, G., and D. Filmer. 2002. "Autonomy, Participation and Learning in Argentine Schools: Findings and Their Implications for Decentralization" World Bank Policy Research Paper Series No. 2766. World Bank, Washington, DC.

Evans, W., and R. Schwab. 1995. "Finishing High School and Starting College: Do Catholic Schools Make a Difference?" *Quarterly Journal of Economics* 110 (4): 941–74.

Galiani, S., P. Gertler, and E. Schargrodsky. 2005. "School Decentralization: Helping the Good Get Better, but Leaving the Rest Behind." Mimeo. Universidad de San Andrés, UC Berkeley, and Universidad Torcuato Di Tella.

González, R. A., and G. Arévalo. 2005. "Subsidized Catholic Schools in Venezuela." In *Private Education and Public Policy in Latin America*, ed. L. Wolff, J. C. Navarro, and P. González. Washington, DC: Project for Educational Revitalization in the Americas.

Hanushek, E. 1994. "Making Schools Work: Improving Performance and Controlling Costs." Brookings Institution Press, Washington, DC.

Heckman, J., H. Ichimura, and P. Todd. 1997. "Matching as an Econometric Evaluation Estimator: Evidence from Evaluating a Job Training Program." *The Review of Economic Studies* 64 (4): 605–54.

Hoenack, S. 1994. "Economics, Organizations and Learning: Research Directions for the Economics of Education." *Economics of Education Review* 13 (2): 147–62.

King, E., and B. Ozler. 2000. "What's Decentralization Got To Do With Learning? Endogenous School Quality and Student Performance in Nicaragua." World Bank Development Research Group, Washington, DC.

Manski, C. 1992. "Educational Choice (Vouchers) and Social Mobility." *Economics of Education Review* 11 (4): 351–69.

Navarro, J. C., and R. de la Cruz. 1998. "Escuelas Federales, Estatales y Sin Fines de Lucro en Venezuela." In *La Organización Marca la Diferencia: Educación y Salud en América Latina*, ed. W. Savedoff. Washington, DC: Inter-American Development Bank.

Pães de Barros, R., and R. Mendonça. 1998. "El Impacto de Tres Innovaciones Institucionales en la Educacion Brasileña" In *La Organización Marca la Diferencia: Educación y Salud en América Latina*, ed. W. Savedoff. Washington, DC: Inter-American Development Bank.

Parker, C. 2005. "Teacher Incentives and Student Achievement in Nicaraguan Autonomous Schools." In *Incentives to Improve Teaching: Lessons from Latin America*, ed. E. Vegas. Washington, DC: World Bank.

Saavedra, J. 1996. "Public and Private Education: Their Relative Impact on Earnings. Evidence from Peruvian Survey Data." Mimeo. GRADE, Lima, Peru.

Savedoff, W. 1998. *La Organización Marca la Diferencia: Educación y Salud en América Latina*. Washington, DC: Inter-American Development Bank.

Sawada, Y., and A. Ragatz. 2005. "Decentralization of Education, Teacher Behavior, and Outcomes: The Case of El Salvador's EDUCO Program." In *Incentives to Improve Teaching: Lessons from Latin America*, ed. E. Vegas. Washington, DC: World Bank.

Vegas, E. 2005. *Incentives to Improve Teaching: Lessons from Latin America*. Washington, DC: World Bank.

CHAPTER 7

Literacy and Numeracy in Faith-Based and Government Schools in Sierra Leone

Quentin Wodon and Yvonne Ying

Introduction

An emerging body of evidence suggests that private schools, including faith-based schools, may provide better education services than public schools (e.g., Allcott and Ortega 2009; Altonji et al. 2005; Asadullah et al. 2009; Cox and Jimenez 1990; Evans and Schwab 1995; González and Arévalo 2005; Hoxby 1994; Hsieh and Urquiola 2006).

In the economic literature, several reasons have been advanced to explain the gains in performance associated with private schools (Epple and Romano 1998; LaRocque and Patrinos 2006; Nechyba 2000; Savas 2000). First, private schools may introduce competition in the education sector and thereby raise overall quality. Second, private providers may have more flexibility than public providers in the management of the schools. Third, to the extent that private providers of education are competitively selected, better providers would emerge in the private as opposed to the public sphere. Fourth, risk sharing between the government and the private sector may also lead to better provision.

The explanations given above for the potentially higher quality of private schools are not likely to hold very well in the context of very poor postconflict African countries. Indeed, most households have very few choices in regard to accessible schooling facilities, so that competition and risk sharing rarely take place. Education provision is not profitable, so that there is no competitive selection of private providers. Finally, flexibility is limited, especially when large faith-based school networks are integrated in the national education systems.

In the African context, faith-based providers are important especially in the provision of education services in conflict-affected countries in which services provided by the state have been weakened by war or strife. In this context, the potential benefit from private faith-based schools could come instead from the dedication that faith-based providers share. As argued by Reinikka and Svensson (forthcoming) in the case of health service provision in Uganda, faith-based providers are less motivated by profit or perks maximization—they seem to be "working for God."

Sierra Leone is one of the African countries in which the market share of faith-based schools is largest (the Democratic Republic of Congo is another case, as shown by Backiny-Yetna and Wodon [2009]). The country's population has suffered from a declining standard of living since the early 1970s, first as a result of poor macroeconomic management and then a civil conflict. With the start of the civil war in the early 1990s, the country plunged into instability. Today, per capita GDP is still below the level reached in the early 1990s.

As a result of the war, Sierra Leone fares poorly in most indicators related to human development and the Millennium Development Goals. For 2005 the country was ranked last in the human development index computed by the United Nations Development Program. Life expectancy at birth was reported to be only 41.8 years. Infant mortality in 2005 was estimated at 170 per 1,000 live births, and under-five mortality at 286 per 1,000. According to the 2005 MICS-III household survey, 31 percent of children under five were underweight, 40 percent stunted, and 9 percent wasted.[1] The adult literacy rate was 34.8 percent, and the combined gross enrollment rate for primary, secondary, and tertiary education was estimated at 44.6 percent.

Since the end of the civil war in 2002, the government and development partners have aimed with substantial success to complete the transition to peace and provide conditions for renewed growth. The government completed its disarmament, demobilization, and reintegration program in 2004. A full poverty reduction strategy was finalized in 2005. In December 2006, Sierra Leone reached the completion point under the Enhanced Heavily Indebted Poor Countries Initiative and gained additional relief under the Multilateral Debt Relief Initiative. Parliamentary and presidential elections were completed in August 2007, with a presidential runoff election in September 2007. The elections, judged to be free and fair, resulted in a transfer of power to the opposition party. These developments have contributed to strong economic growth and poverty reduction in recent years.

As a result of historical factors (schools have long been established by missionaries and more recently by Muslim groups) as well as a weak state due to civil conflict, more than half of all students today attend faith-based schools. As noted by Nishimuko (2008), government schools are managed by the Ministry of Education, Sports and Technology (MEST) and often owned by the local government and district council. Government-assisted schools tend to be faith-based and benefit from essentially the same government subsidies as government schools (through teacher salaries and the provision of teaching materials). By contrast, private schools that are not faith-based do not benefit from such subsidies.

There are a number of potential advantages in having faith-based organizations (FBOs) providing education services. As noted by Belshaw (2005), FBOs have a long-term commitment to their communities and they often reach out to the poorest members of the community. Through links to sister organizations in other countries, they may benefit from outside funding and expertise. Faith-based schools often emphasize values of respect and consideration for others. In addition, religious leaders often have a moral authority that helps in mobilizing the community's resources around the schools.[2] But faith-based schools may also suffer from weaknesses, especially if they place the pursuit of their religious mandate ahead of the needs of students in regard to what they need to learn to be successful in today's world.

Two recent studies completed by the World Bank (2007, 2008) provide a basic diagnostic of the education system in Sierra Leone. The studies suggest that, because of its postconflict status, Sierra Leone stands out in comparison with other countries in a number of areas. First, there are large differences between net and gross enrollment rates because many older children have returned to school since the end of the conflict. Second, cost remains the main reason for never having gone to school or not continuing one's education. Third, satisfaction rates with the services received are low in all types of schools. The main complaints are the lack of books or supplies, the high fees that have to be paid, and the fact that facilities are in poor condition. Yet both studies provide only very limited information on the role played by faith-based providers in education and on the comparative performance of faith-based and government schools.

In this chapter, our objective is to provide a comparative assessment of the performance of faith-based and public schools using data from the 2004 Sierra Leone Integrated Household Survey (SLIHS). According to the survey, about one-third of primary school students attend government schools. More than half of the students are in faith-based government-assisted schools. The rest of the students are mainly in private nonsubsidized schools. The SLIHS data can be used to analyze whom various types of schools serve (i.e., whether faith-based schools reach the poor more than do government schools), as well as whether children can read and write in English, whether they can compute, and whether they have repeated a grade. The data on literacy and numeracy are subjective assessments made by household heads concerning the abilities of their children and are thereby substantially less precise than test scores. But they are nevertheless useful indicators to assess the comparative performance of various types of schools.

In what follows we first provide basic statistics on the market share of faith-based providers in Sierra Leone and the measures of performance that can be obtained from the SLIHS survey. Next, we use instrumental variable econometric techniques to assess whether faith-based schools achieve better outcomes for their students than public schools, taking into account the possibility of endogenous choice of school type by parents. We do find that, as expected, faith-based schools do perform better, at least in some dimensions, than public government schools, and that the differences between the two types of schools are important. A brief conclusion follows.

Basic Statistics

As in other Anglophone countries in West Africa, Sierra Leone's education system consists of four main levels: primary schools (six years of study), junior secondary schools (three years), senior secondary schools (three years), and tertiary education. In this chapter, we focus on primary and secondary education indicators (with secondary education combining the junior and senior levels), given that the share of youths pursuing post-secondary education is very low.

Table 7.1 provides the market shares of various types of providers by quintile of per capita consumption (with the first quintile, "Q1," representing the poorest 20 percent of the population, and the top quintile, "Q5," the richest 20 percent). Given that the proportion of the population in

Table 7.1   Market Share of School Providers by Level and Quintile of Consumption

	% students in Q1	% students in Q2	% students in Q3	% students in Q4	% students in Q5	% of all students	% female students
Primary schools							
Rural							
Government	21.0	20.2	24.9	20.4	13.5	28.9	47.9
Local government	62.4	18.7	15.3	2.4	1.2	2.6	36.5
Faith-based	33.1	24.2	23.4	14.0	5.3	57.7	52.3
NGO	41.1	29.2	11.1	2.1	16.5	0.9	33.7
Private	23.3	19.6	3.6	26.8	26.6	4.4	49.2
Other	47.5	41.2	9.1	2.3	0.0	5.5	37.8
Total	30.8	23.7	21.9	15.4	8.3	100.0	49.5
Urban							
Government	11.9	13.7	16.8	28.2	29.3	38.2	47.4
Local government	8.8	23.7	26.0	22.6	18.8	8.0	51.3
Faith-based	10.5	17.5	25.9	25.2	20.9	45.6	50.7
NGO	0.0	0.0	25.2	74.8	0.0	0.3	72.2
Private	1.9	6.3	8.4	32.2	51.3	8.0	51.8
Other	0.0	40.0	0.0	60.0	0.0	0.0	0.0
Total	10.2	15.6	21.1	26.8	26.3	100.0	49.6
Secondary schools							
Rural							
Government	10.7	17.9	21.5	17.9	32.1	45.4	27.8
Local government	13.0	78.5	0.0	0.0	8.5	1.6	8.5
Faith-based	24.9	17.9	21.1	22.1	14.0	48.3	36.0
NGO	0.0	0.0	0.0	0.0	100.0	1.8	100.0
Private	0.0	0.0	0.0	15.9	84.1	3.0	84.1
Total	17.0	18.0	19.9	19.3	25.8	100.0	34.5
Urban							
Government	1.6	5.3	10.4	26.5	56.2	53.4	60.5
Local government	11.6	1.5	1.6	44.6	40.8	2.5	44.9
Faith-based	7.5	16.7	17.8	22.6	35.5	41.1	45.1
NGO	0.0	24.0	0.0	0.0	76.0	0.6	71.6
Private	0.0	0.0	1.9	20.0	78.1	2.5	27.7
Total	4.2	9.9	12.9	25.0	48.0	100.0	53.1

Source: Authors' estimation using 2003–04 SLIHS.

poverty is at about 64 percent, the first three quintiles can be considered as representing the poor. Faith-based providers account for 58 percent of all primary school students in rural areas and 46 percent in urban areas. In secondary schools, faith-based providers account for 48 percent of students in rural areas and 41 percent in urban areas. Government schools have a market share similar to that of faith-based schools at the secondary level, but at the primary level, government schools account for only 29 percent of students in rural areas and 38 percent in urban areas.

Faith-based schools tend to serve the poor more than government schools in rural areas. For example, 33 percent of students in faith-based schools belong to the poorest quintile, versus only 5 percent to the richest quintile. For government schools, the proportions are 21 percent in the poorest quintile and 14 percent in the richest quintile. In urban areas, the distributional pattern is less clear-cut, with faith-based schools overrepresented in the middle quintile, but still overall serving the poor more than other schools. Because more than two-thirds of the population lives in rural areas, faith-based schools are especially important for the poor.

Faith-based schools also have a larger share of female students than government schools. Indeed, in primary schools in rural areas girls account for 52 percent of all students in faith-based schools (51 percent in urban areas), versus 48 percent of all students in government schools (47 percent in urban areas; this last difference is not statistically significant). At the secondary level, faith-based schools have a higher proportion of female students than government schools, but that is not the case in urban areas.

Beyond government and faith-based schools, the survey also identifies local government, NGO, private, and other schools, but their market shares are much lower than those observed for government and faith-based schools, which together account for 85 in 100 students at the primary level and an even higher proportion at the secondary level. Although this is not shown in table 7.1, the data suggest that faith-based schools do not discriminate among their students in regard to faith, as noted also by Nishimuko (2008). In what follows, we will focus on a comparison of performance indicators only for government and faith-based schools, given that private schools are not subsidized and tend to cater to a different set of students by charging higher fees.

To compare the performance of faith-based and government schools, we rely on four indicators: (1) whether students can read English, (2) whether students can write in English, (3) whether students can perform simple computations, and (4) whether students have repeated a grade. Table 7.2 provides summary statistics on these four performance indicators among all children enrolled in school. Only a small minority of the students can read or write in English in primary schools, but the proportion is very high in secondary schools. About a third of the students can perform simple computations in primary schools, and again the proportion

Table 7.2   School Performance Indicators

	% of students who can read English	% of students who can write in English	% of students who can compute	% of students who repeat the grade
Primary schools				
Rural				
Government	8.0	7.6	30.5	10.6
Faith-based	6.7	2.3	34.0	14.9
Total	6.9	4.2	32.5	13.5
Urban				
Government	27.8	26.5	43.0	10.7
Faith-based	12.5	10.7	22.7	16.3
Total	20.9	19.1	32.3	14.2
Secondary schools				
Rural				
Government	98.2	95.1	97.9	5.0
Faith-based	93.5	94.5	88.9	6.0
Total	95.4	94.6	93.2	5.2
Urban				
Government	97.4	94.4	94.5	8.2
Faith-based	98.8	97.6	95.3	9.6
Total	96.9	94.6	94.0	9.6

Source: Authors' estimation using 2003–04 SLIHS.

is very high in secondary schools. About one in six children has repeated a grade in primary school, and the proportion is lower in secondary than in primary schools.

Looking at the data in table 7.2, one could be led to believe that government schools perform better than faith-based schools. Indeed, for primary schools in both urban and rural areas, a higher proportion of students in government schools can read and write in English, and the repetition rate is lower in government schools. Faith-based schools seem to perform better only in regard to the share of students who can compute in rural primary schools, whereas in urban areas, the advantage enjoyed by government schools is large. At the secondary level, the differences are smaller between both types of schools, although rural students in government schools seem to perform slightly better.

However, such simple comparisons of performance between the two types of schools do not account for the fact that there are potentially important differences in the types of students that enroll in government and faith-based schools. As mentioned earlier, students enrolled in faith-based schools tend to be from significantly poorer backgrounds than students in government schools. Essentially, this is the result of a higher concentration of faith-based schools in the poorest parts of the country, which were also severely affected by the civil conflict of the 1990s. Poorer students are likely to perform less well in school for a wide range of reasons. They may have to miss school more often or may have less time to study because of the need to contribute to household livelihood. Their parents are also less likely to be well educated and thereby to coach them. They may live farther away from schools, which makes studying and going to school harder. Just as important, they are likely to live in areas in which the quality of schooling is lower, as a result of, for example, teachers having lower qualifications and higher pupil-to-teacher ratios in the poorest districts (Wodon and Ye 2009). The key question is whether controlling for the characteristics of the students and of their geographic areas, faith-based schools perform better or worse than government schools. To answer that question, we turn in the next section to an econometric analysis of the SLIHS data.

Econometric Analysis

Our technique for assessing the variables related to performance is simple. We estimate binary outcome (probit) models on whether a child can read or write, can compute, and has repeated a grade, using as explanatory variables a large number of child, household, and geographic characteristics, including whether or not the child is in a faith-based or government school. However, the choice of school for a child (faith-based or government) can itself depend on the child's performance, which we measure here as reading, writing, and computing abilities, and repetition of a grade (see box 7.1). To avoid the potential problems induced by this two-way dependence between performance as the dependent variable and school choice as an explanatory variable, we instrument the choice of the type of school the child goes to using the leave-out mean share of the students in the child's geographic area that are going to faith-based schools. The child's geographic area is identified through the primary sampling unit to which the household belongs in the survey (each primary sampling unit includes typically between 20 and 30 households). We use the leave-out mean participation rate in faith-based school, which does not take into account whether the child, or any child in the same household, attends that type of school.

Box 7.1

Leave-out Means and Instrumental Variables

Leave-out means. Assume we want to compute the leave-out share (mean) of children attending school. We first define the way observations in a survey are to be grouped (alternatives include neighborhoods, counties, and enumeration areas, among others), and then for every group and for each observation in the group, we compute the share of children attending school in the group, excluding the observation being analyzed. The share computed as described is known as the leave-out mean. Note that each observation in the same group might have a different value for the leave-out mean. When computing the leave-out shares in this chapter, we exclude all children in the same household. This strategy of identifying the outcome regression through a leave-out mean Primary Sampling Unit (PSU)–level variable affecting the choice of an individual was used among others by Ravallion and Wodon (2001) in their work on schooling and child labor in Bangladesh and by Wodon (2000) in work on the impact of low-income energy policies on the probability of electricity disconnection in France.

Instrumental variables technique. If the dependent and at least one of the explanatory variables cause each other (known as endogeneity bias), standard linear regression models would produce estimates that are inconsistent and biased. If it is possible to find a variable that is correlated with the explanatory variable (conditioning on the other explanatory variables) that is caused by the dependent variable (endogenous regressor), and not correlated with the dependent variable, then we can use it as an instrument in the estimation to produce consistent estimates. In this chapter, we use the leave-out share of the students that attend a faith-based school in the primary sampling unit as an instrument of the school choice as an explanatory variable for student performance. We believe the leave-out share is correlated with school choice because it is an indication of the density of faith-based schools in the vicinity of the household, although it is unlikely to be correlated with learning outcomes beyond the fact that it affects the likelihood of going to a specific type of school.

Four binary outcome (probit) models have to be estimated, one for each performance measure, and the analysis is undertaken on the sample of children who are attending faith-based schools and non-faith-based schools (this includes both government and non-government schools). The results are presented in table A7.1 and A7.2 for primary schools (see annex).

The explanatory variables we use for the students' performance are (1) the type of school the child attends (this variable is instrumented as explained above to avoid endogeneity issues); (2) the grade the child is attending (with the first grade of the cycle being the reference category); (3) the time it takes for the child to go to school and the square of that time; (4) the characteristics of the child—age of the child and the age squared, sex of the child, whether the child has both parents out of his or her home, or only the mother or father not at home; (5) the geographic location of the child according to urban or rural status and the four main regions in the country (with the southern region as the reference category); (6) the religion of the child (with Muslim being the reference category); (7) the rank of the child in the household in regard to the child's age in comparison with other children; (8) the migration status of the child; (9) the household demographic variables—household size and whether the household head is male or female; (10) the education level of the father of the child (none, primary, secondary, or postsecondary) and the same variables for the mother of the child; and (11) the occupation of the father and the mother (farming is the reference category).

We concentrate now on the results for primary schools. The key variable of interest is the impact of the type of school the child attends on performance measured by literacy and numeracy. Controlling for other characteristics, attending a faith-based school increases performance, with the impact strongly statistically significant for numeracy and marginally significant for reading English. The impact is not statistically significant for writing in English and for the probability of repetition.

Having statistical significance, what matters is the magnitude of the effect. Using the results from our estimations, one can predict the increase in the probability of numeracy and ability to read English for a child obtained from shifting from a non-faith-based school to a faith-based school.[3] For numeracy, the probability of being able to compute increases from 39.1 percent to 46.6 percent. For the ability to read English, the probability increases from 20.4 percent to 24.3 percent. Thus, the econometric analysis corrects the (faulty) first impression that could have been generated by a simple look at the basic statistics in table 7.2, in which without proper controls it appeared that faith-based schools had a lower performance than government schools. The reverse is actually the case.

The results from the estimations also provide a number of other interesting findings for primary schools. As expected, if a child is in a higher grade, the likelihood of being able to read or write a letter in English and the likelihood of being able to perform a simple computation are higher. A higher distance to the school reduces the likelihood of being able to read English. The age and gender of the child do not affect literacy and numeracy controlling for the other variables (the age is already captured indirectly by the grade the child is in). Children in the western region, which is the least poor, tend to have higher rates of literacy and numeracy; whereas in the eastern region, which is the poorest and was most affected by conflict, children have the lowest rate of numeracy controlling for other characteristics (although the East does better than the South on literacy).[4] Christians, including Catholics, tend to do better than Muslim children, perhaps because of a stronger tradition of emphasis placed on education among Christian households. When the effects of the mother's education are statistically significant, they are positive, as expected. However, the father's education is not statistically significant (in the case of writing in English, a student whose father's education is at the secondary school level fares less well than children with fathers having no education). The mother's occupation significantly affects a child's achievements in both numeracy and literacy. That is, if the mother's occupation is in nonfarming sectors, the child does better in calculation and reading and writing in English.

Very similar models were estimated for secondary school students (see table A7.2 in the annex). The regressions for secondary school students have slightly more aggregated categories for a few of the explanatory variables.[5] Fewer variables are statistically significant, which is not surprising given that the variance in achievement tends to be smaller (most children at that stage of their studies know how to read or write in English and can perform simple computations). We do however find again a statistically significant and positive impact of attending a faith-based school on numeracy and writing in English. The impact of the type of school attended on reading English was found not to be statistically significant.

Conclusion

The objective of this chapter was to provide a comparative assessment of the performance of faith-based and government school students in Sierra Leone on literacy and numeracy. Simple basic statistics suggest slightly lower performance in faith-based schools than in government schools, but faith-based schools tend to serve a much more disadvantaged population than government schools. After controlling for child and household characteristics, and after taking into account the potential endogeneity of school choice depending on the performance of the student, we found that actually faith-based schools perform slightly better than government schools—this effect is statistically significant, especially in primary school, but its magnitude is very small. Still, given the fact that faith-based schools serve disadvantaged students with a focus on poor rural areas, have a very large market share especially at the primary level, and perform at least as well as government schools once appropriate controls are taken into account, the empirical results provided in this chapter are supportive of the financial support provided by the state to those schools.

Annex: Regression Results

Table A7.1   Correlates of Student Performance in Primary Schools—Numeracy and Literacy (Reading)

	Numeracy			Literacy (read English)		
	Coef.		Std. err.	Coef.		Std. err.
At religious school, instrumented	0.2443	***	0.0728	0.2151	**	0.1039
School grade (omit grade 1)						
Grade 2	0.3655	***	0.0677	0.1962		0.1377
Grade 3	0.7848	***	0.0727	0.8089	***	0.1332
Grade 4	0.9702	***	0.0801	1.0489	***	0.1399
Grade 5	1.2394	***	0.0874	1.5006	***	0.1439
Grade 6	1.8356	***	0.1026	2.2071	***	0.1509
Time to school, minutes	−0.0031	***	0.0012	−0.0022		0.0016
Time to school square, minutes	0.0000		0.0000	0.0000		0.0000
Age	−0.2335		0.5625	−0.2533		0.8154
Age square	0.0054		0.0096	0.0087		0.0140
Female	0.0229		0.0417	0.0233		0.0558
Rural	0.0749		0.0490	−0.0204		0.0641
Region (omit South)						
East	−0.5902	***	0.0576	0.3470	***	0.0767
North	0.2929	***	0.0505	0.0768		0.0761
West	0.2894	***	0.0783	1.3170	***	0.0970
Religious (omit Muslim)						
Catholic	0.1815	***	0.0668	−0.0008		0.0898
Other Christians	0.1303	**	0.0556	0.1809	***	0.0691
Other religious	0.2464	*	0.1482	−0.1964		0.2243
Child rank position	0.0002		0.0005	0.0002		0.0007
Child of household head	0.0878	*	0.0497	−0.0093		0.0690

(continued)

111

Table A7.1 Correlates of Student Performance in Primary Schools—Numeracy and Literacy (Reading) *(Continued)*

	Numeracy		Literacy (read English)		
	Coef.	Std. err.	Coef.		Std. err.
Migration (omit never move)					
Moved	-0.0291	0.1203	-0.2094	*	0.1269
Move data missing	0.1364	0.1154	0.2134		0.1301
Household size	0.0103	0.0098	0.0087		0.0128
Female household head	-0.0091	0.0161	-0.0091		0.0210
Father education (omit no education)					
Primary	-0.0710	0.0857	-0.0914		0.1180
Secondary	-0.0438	0.0864	-0.1526		0.1162
Postsecondary	0.1100	0.0856	0.1269		0.1068
Koran	-0.0390	0.0931	-0.1300		0.1355
Mother education (omit no education)					
Primary	-0.1057	0.0875	0.0652		0.1128
Secondary	0.1409	0.0927	0.2541	**	0.1099
Postsecondary	0.3105 **	0.1494	0.1361		0.1781
Koran	0.1414	0.2835	-0.2322		0.4908
Father occupation (omit farming)					
Trade	0.0583	0.1003	-0.0682		0.1308
Other	-0.0821	0.0734	0.0296		0.0906
Mother occupation (omit farming)					
Trade	0.1655 **	0.0700	0.1557	*	0.0878
Clerical	0.1303	0.3469	0.6404	*	0.3530
Construction	1.5032 **	0.6278	0.8740		0.5682
Professional	-0.2411	0.2298	-0.0489		0.2761
Other	-0.0523	0.0917	0.1184		0.1092
Constant	-1.4131	0.9590	-2.6355	*	1.3982

Source: Authors' estimation using 2003–04 SLIHS.

Note: *** indicates statistical significance at .01 percent level; ** at .05 percent level, and * at .1 percent level.

Table A7.2 Correlates of Student Performance in Primary Schools—Literacy (Writing) and Repetition

	Literacy (write in English)			Repetition		
	Coef.		Std. err.	Coef.		Std. err.
At religious school, instrumented	−0.1378		0.1151	0.1256		0.0815
School grade (omit grade 1)						
Grade 2	0.1357		0.1464	0.0418		0.0730
Grade 3	0.4293	***	0.1472	0.0430		0.0792
Grade 4	0.7340	***	0.1535	0.0441		0.0871
Grade 5	1.3707	***	0.1559	−0.0052		0.0946
Grade 6	2.1796	***	0.1624	−0.0604		0.1053
Time to school, minutes	−0.0028		0.0018	0.0007		0.0013
Time to school square, minutes	0.0000		0.0000	0.0000		0.0000
Age	−0.0869		0.8974	0.3810		0.6303
Age square	0.0031		0.0154	−0.0073		0.0108
Female	−0.0977		0.0620	0.0576		0.0456
Rural	−0.0656		0.0712	−0.1160	**	0.0530
Region (omit South)						
East	0.2048	**	0.0860	0.1919	***	0.0611
North	0.0372		0.0848	0.1340	**	0.0585
West	1.3134	***	0.1029	0.1519	*	0.0858
Religious (omit Muslim)						
Catholic	0.0176		0.0994	−0.0133		0.0742
Other Christians	0.1402	*	0.0761	0.1938	***	0.0582
Other religious	0.0937		0.2271	−0.0313		0.1611
Child rank position	0.0001		0.0008	−0.0002		0.0006
Child of household head	0.0246		0.0771	−0.0974	*	0.0544

(continued)

Table A7.2 Correlates of Student Performance in Primary Schools—Literacy (Writing) and Repetition (Continued)

	Literacy (write in English)			Repetition		
	Coef.		Std. err.	Coef.		Std. err.
Migration (omit never move)						
Moved	−0.2471	*	0.1333	0.0638		0.1244
Move data missing	−0.0196		0.1373	0.2090	*	0.1211
Household size	0.0059		0.0141	−0.0062		0.0110
Female household head	−0.0090		0.0231	−0.0013		0.0180
Father education (omit no education)						
Primary	−0.1629		0.1327	0.0190		0.0911
Secondary	−0.3162	**	0.1332	0.0555		0.0905
Postsecondary	0.1002		0.1157	−0.1243		0.0943
Koran	−0.2165		0.1563	−0.0518		0.1062
Mother education (omit no education)						
Primary	0.0934		0.1248	0.1941	**	0.0897
Secondary	0.3510	***	0.1159	0.0401		0.0996
Postsecondary	0.2956		0.1850	0.1387		0.1637
Koran	−0.0081		0.4803	0.4022		0.2900
Father occupation (omit farming)						
Trade	−0.2060		0.1490	0.1356		0.1063
Other	0.0436		0.0993	0.0640		0.0773
Mother occupation (omit farming)						
Trade	0.1348		0.0959	0.1328	*	0.0744
Clerical	0.7051	**	0.3534	−0.5542		0.4305
Construction	0.7081		0.6120	–		
Professional	−0.0258		0.2880	0.0820		0.2390
Other	0.1482		0.1179	−0.1659	*	0.1005
Constant	−2.5707	*	1.5376	−2.9407	***	1.0784

Source: Authors' estimation using 2003–04 SLIHS.

Note: Because of the problem of perfect prediction in the probit regression for repetition for mother's occupation in construction, the construction occupation is included in mother's occupation in other sectors. Note: *** indicates statistical significance at .01 percent level; ** at .05 percent level, and * at .1 percent level

Notes

1. Underweight refers to cases in which a child's weight is too low given the child's age, stunted refers to a child's height being too low given the child's age, and wasted refers to a child's weight being too low given the child's height.

2. As noted by Nishimuko (2008), the role of faith leaders and organizations in Sierra Leone has included among others: "1) Obtaining land for school construction; 2) Construction and rehabilitation of schools; 3) Provision of vehicles, furniture, teaching learning materials from time to time; 4) Offering scholarships to teachers for further study; 5) Offering scholarship to pupils; 6) Regularly visiting schools to monitor; 7) Recruitment of teachers; 8) Training of Arabic teachers (in Islamic schools) and offering in-service training for Religious Moral Education; 9) Producing religious literature for schools and churches or mosques; 10) Occasionally making up teachers' salaries when teachers have not been paid by the government; 11) Sensitizing parents at churches or mosques so that they send their children to schools; and 12) Establishing and disseminating a code of conduct to maintain morality in schools and communities."

3. We use results on numeracy and ability to read English as these are the outcomes for which the type of school attended has a statistically significant impact.

4. According to the World Bank (2008), the poverty head count at the national level was 66 percent. In the western region, which includes the capital of Sierra Leone, Freetown, the head count was at 29 percent. In the northern region, the head count was at 78 percent, versus 61 percent in the southern region and 84 percent in the eastern region.

5. This is to avoid perfect predictions due to the fact that the sample of students in secondary schools is smaller than that for primary schools.

References

Allcott, H., and D. E. Ortega. 2009. "The Performance of Decentralized School Systems: Evidence from Fe y Alegría in Venezuela." In *Emerging Evidence on Private Participation in Education: Vouchers and Faith-Based Providers*, ed. F. Barrera-Osorio, H. A. Patrinos, and Q. Wodon. Washington, DC: World Bank.

Asadullah, M. N., N. Chaudhury, and A. Dar. 2009. "Student Achievement in Religious and Secular Secondary Schools in Bangladesh." In *Emerging Evidence on Private Participation in Education: Vouchers and Faith-Based Providers*, ed. F. Barrera-Osorio, H. A. Patrinos, and Q. Wodon. Washington, DC: World Bank.

Altonji, J. G., T. E. Elder, and C. R. Taber. 2005. "An Evaluation of Instrumental Variable Strategies for Estimating the Effects of Catholic Schooling." *Journal of Human Resources* 40 (4): 791–821.

Backiny-Yetna, P., and Q. Wodon. 2009. "Comparing Faith-Based and Government Schools in the Democratic Republic of Congo." In *Emerging Evidence on Private Participation in Education: Vouchers and Faith-Based Providers*, ed. F. Barrera-Osorio, H. A. Patrinos, and Q. Wodon. Washington, DC: World Bank.

Belshaw, D. 2005. "Enhancing the Development Capability of Civil Society Organisations, with Particular Reference to Christian Faith-based Organisations (FBOs)." In *Reclaiming Development: Assessing the Contributions of Non-Governmental Organisations to Development Alternatives.* London: Economic and Social Research Council Global Poverty Research Group.

Cox, D., and E. Jimenez. 1990. "The Relative Effectiveness of Private and Public Schools: Evidence from two Developing Countries." *Journal of Development Economics* 34 (1–2): 99–121.

Epple, D., and R. E. Romano. 1998. "Competition between Private and Public Schools, Vouchers, and Peer-Group Effects." *American Economic Review* 88 (1): 33–62.

Evans, W., and R. Schwab. 1995. "Finishing High School and Starting College: Do Catholic Schools Make a Difference?" *Quarterly Journal of Economics* 110 (4): 941–74.

González, R. A., and G. Arévalo. 2005. "Subsidized Catholic Schools in Venezuela." In *Private Education and Public Policy in Latin America*, ed. L. Wolff, J. C. Navarro, and P. González. Washington, DC: Project For Educational Revitalization in the Americas.

Hsieh, C., and M. Urquiola. 2006. "The Effects of Generalized School Choice on Achievement and Stratification: Evidence from Chile's School Voucher Program." *Journal of Public Economics* 90: 1477–1503.

Hoxby, C. M. 1994. "Do Private Schools Provide Competition for Public Schools?" NBER (National Bureau of Economic Research) Working Paper 4978. NBER, Cambridge, MA.

LaRocque, N., and H. Patrinos. 2006. "Choice and Contracting Mechanisms in the Education Sector." Mimeo. World Bank, Washington, DC.

Nechyba, T. J. 2000. "Mobility, Targeting and Private School Vouchers." *American Economic Review* 90 (1): 130–46.

Nishimuko, M. 2008. "The Role of Faith-Based Organizations in Building Democratic Process: Achieving Universal Primary Education in Sierra Leone." *International Journal of Social Science* 3 (3): 172–79.

Ravallion M., and Q. Wodon. 2000. "Does Child Labor Displace Schooling? Evidence on Behavioral Responses to an Enrollment Subsidy." *Economic Journal* 110: C158–75.

Reinikka, R., and J. Svensson. Forthcoming. "Working for God? Evidence from a Change in Financing of Not-for-Profit Health Care Providers in Uganda." *Journal of the European Economic Association.*

Savas, E. S 2000. *Privatization and Public-Private Partnerships.* New York: Chatham House Publishers.

Wodon Q. 2000. "Low Income Energy Assistance and Disconnection in France." *Applied Economics Letters* 7: 775–79.

Wodon, Q., and X. Ye. 2009. "Needs and Cost-Adjusted Benefit Incidence: Education in Sierra Leone." Mimeo. World Bank, Washington, DC.

World Bank. 2007. "Education in Sierra Leone: Present Challenges, Future Opportunities." Africa Human Development Series, World Bank, Washington, DC.

———. 2008. "Sierra Leone: Poverty Diagnostic." Report No. 44082-SL. World Bank, Washington, DC.

CHAPTER 8

Comparing the Performance of Faith-Based and Government Schools in the Democratic Republic of Congo

Prospere Backiny-Yetna and Quentin Wodon

Introduction

To the extent that faith-based (and more generally nonprofit) providers of education or health services are altruistic (Reinikka and Svensson forthcoming), we could expect that they would provide better services for the poor than public providers. This would be important for African postconflict countries in which faith-based and alternative service providers of education play a large role (e.g., Bekalo et al. 2003; Dennis and Fentiman 2007; Wodon and Ying 2009).

As noted in the previous chapter, there is some evidence that faith-based and nonprofit service providers offer services of good quality and often more so than public schools (e.g., Allcott and Ortega 2009; Asadullah et al. 2009; Altonji et al. 2005; Cox and Jimenez 1990; Evans and Schwab 1995; González and Arévalo 2005; Hoxby 1994; Hsieh and Urquiola 2006). However, in extremely poor countries in which state education systems are especially fragile, in which an overwhelming majority of students attend faith-based schools, and in which because of a lack of public financing the cost of education is essentially borne by parents whether the children go to public or private schools, differences between faith-based and public schools could be rather limited.

The Democratic Republic of Congo is such a country. The aftermath of independence was a period of political instability in the Democratic Republic of Congo, but the country was relatively peaceful and growing, creating a strong demand for education. From the mid-1960s to the mid-1970s, school enrollment grew, fueled not only by population growth but also by gains in enrollment rates, at an annual rate of 5 percent in primary, 19 percent in secondary, and 24 percent in tertiary education (World Bank 2005). The growth in enrollment decelerated during the economic crisis period that started in the mid-1970s and lasted for two decades (this crisis was triggered by a deterioration in trade caused by a decline in copper prices). Yet it was only after 1995, during a period marked by the end of the 32-year Mobutu regime and the start of a civil war, that primary enrollment started to decrease.

In the decade from 1995 to 2004, the Democratic Republic of Congo suffered from a long civil war that had a devastating effect on the economy and the population (estimates of the number of deaths range from 3 to 5.5 million people). In part as a result of this civil war, in 2005 more than 7 in 10 people lived in poverty (World Bank 2008). The conflict also led to dramatic losses in human development indicators, including a decline in primary enrollment rates and stagnation in secondary enrollment rates, something that had not been observed before (World Bank 2005).

Our objective in this chapter is to conduct an analysis of the comparative performance of faith-based and public schools in the Democratic Republic of Congo. After providing some background on the education system in the Democratic Republic of Congo, we use the nationally representative 1-2-3 survey of 2004–05 to analyze the market share of various types of education providers and whom these providers serve. Next, we use econometric methods to assess whether faith-based providers have a better performance, as measured by literacy and dropout rates, than government schools, taking into account the possibility of endogenous choice of school type by parents. The data on literacy are subjective assessments made by household heads concerning the abilities of their children and are thereby substantially less precise than test scores, but nevertheless useful indicators to assess the comparative performance of various types of schools. We find that faith-based schools perform slightly better at least in some dimensions than government schools, but the differences between the two types of schools are small, and they are not statistically significant in the case of the Democratic Republic of Congo.

Background on the Education Sector

Primary and secondary education in the Democratic Republic of Congo is provided by three types of schools: government schools (*écoles non-conventionées*), faith-based schools (*écoles conventionnées*), and private schools. Both government and faith-based schools receive subsidies and are considered public schools. By contrast, private schools do not benefit from state support. In this chapter, we are concerned with the performance of publicly supported education, which includes public and faith-based schools. The term "publicly supported," although correct, is somewhat of a misnomer in the Democratic Republic of Congo, given the fact that most of the costs of education in the country today are borne by households. As discussed in a World Bank (2005) report, public financing for education has declined substantially since 1986, and as a result public funding for education is very limited. This means that most of the costs of education are borne by parents.

Administratively, between 1997 and 2003, a single Ministry for Education was in charge of primary, secondary, and tertiary education, as well as scientific research. After 2003, the ministry was split in two, with primary, secondary, and professional education being under the supervision of the Ministère de l'Enseignement Primaire, Secondaire, et Professionel (MEPSP) and higher education and scientific research under the supervision of the Ministère de l'Enseignement Supérieur et Universitaire (MESU). Yet as noted by the World Bank (2005), the relationship between the government and religious institutions has not been clearly defined. Private schools, including religious schools, which provide about half of all education services in the country, were nationalized in 1974, but only for three years after which the government entered into a "convention" with the four major religious organizations (Roman Catholic, Protestant, Kimbanguiste, and Islamic). The convention stipulates that faith-based schools must follow the public curriculum and norms on class size, teacher qualifications and salaries, and system of student assessment. In principle, the schools belong to the state even if they are managed by religious organizations. A 1986 law that gave broad authority to the Ministry of Education does not mention the religious school networks, even though a National Council of Education with representation from both the government and the religious networks was later created to coordinate national policy.

In practice, each religious network has its own structure to manage its schools. Each network also has to rely for the most part on its own resources to pay for the services provided. Through various levies, parents provide the bulk of funding, among others for teachers' salaries. Most religious networks have limited ability to provide additional funding. Hence faith-based schools and government schools are in the same situation of relying on parental fees for teacher salaries, with even more limited funding for building new schools or improving existing schools. This also means that the quality of education is low. For example, most children in the fourth grade of primary school have acquired only limited language skills, such as associating words and pictures.

The issues of cost and quality were also documented in a poverty assessment completed at the World Bank (2008). The data confirmed that the private cost of education was very high, especially for the poor, so that affordability issues repeatedly came up as the main reason for not sending children to school, not maintaining them in school regularly, or having them drop out. Two-thirds of potential users of schools found the costs of private schools excessive. The perception concerning publicly funded schools (whether faith-based or government schools) was less extreme, but still a fourth of potential users found costs excessive (27 percent for the *conventionnées* and 22 percent for government schools). Still, despite the high cost of schooling, most households choose their school on the basis of quality (58 percent of parents), as opposed to proximity (23 percent) or cost (16 percent). Among the poor and in rural areas, proximity is a more important limiting factor in regard to the available choice of schools. In urban areas and among better-off households, more weight is placed on quality. Interestingly, slightly more than two-thirds of potential users suggest that the costs of schooling are legitimate to obtain a good education (paying such costs is considered to be a duty for parents).

As for the poor quality of education, it is related to a range of factors. Three-quarters of the school infrastructure is more than 20 years old. Despite norms limiting class size, nearly 40 percent of students in the first grade study in overcrowded classes (class sizes decrease in higher grades as a result of high dropout rates). Appropriate textbooks and instructional materials are missing, and the preparation of new books is not undertaken because of lack of funding. Low-cost instructional aid kits sold to schools and teachers in Kinshasa cannot be supplied in the interior of the country because of logistical problems. As a result of these problems, test scores are low. Under a pilot program, tests were administered in three academic years to 5,000 students in 100 schools (50 target schools receiving assistance form UNICEF and 50 comparator schools receiving no inputs). Average scores for French and mathematics were below 50 percent. Students in target schools (receiving assistance) scored somewhat higher, but the differences were small versus comparator schools. Still, quality did improve over time in both types of schools, with larger improvements in target schools, particularly in French. This suggests that gains can be made, but substantial efforts are needed.

Basic Statistics

This section provides basic statistics on the role of public, private faith-based, and other service providers of education in the Democratic Republic of Congo using the nationally representative 1-2-3 survey. The Democratic Republic of Congo's education system consists of three main levels: primary schools (six years of study), secondary schools (six years), and tertiary education. In this chapter, we focus on primary education indicators. Table 8.1 provides the market shares of various types of providers by quintile of per capita consumption (with the first quintile, "Q1," representing the poorest 20 percent of the population, and the top quintile, "Q5," the richest 20 percent). Given that the proportion of the population in poverty is above 70 percent, the first four quintiles can be considered as representing the poor, or at least households that are vulnerable to poverty.

Faith-based providers account for almost 79 percent of all primary school students in rural areas and 51 percent in urban areas (70 percent

Table 8.1   School Enrollment in Primary School by Quintile

	Q1	Q2	Q3	Q4	Q5	All
Urban						
Public	16.6	20.6	18.5	22.4	21.9	100.0
Religious	18.6	20.0	18.7	21.9	20.8	100.0
Private	9.1	14.3	14.8	27.6	34.2	100.0
All	15.6	18.6	17.6	23.5	24.6	100.0
Rural						
Public	27.8	21.2	20.8	19.9	10.3	100.0
Religious	24.9	23.4	21.5	17.4	12.7	100.0
Private	28.0	19.6	21.8	12.2	18.3	100.0
All	25.6	22.9	21.4	17.6	12.5	100.0
Congo, Dem. Rep. of						
Public	23.4	21.0	19.9	20.9	14.9	100.0
Religious	23.5	22.6	20.9	18.5	14.6	100.0
Private	14.3	15.8	16.7	23.3	29.9	100.0
All	22.4	21.5	20.2	19.5	16.4	100.0

Source: Authors' calculations using 1-2-3 survey, Democratic Republic of Congo, 2005.

at the national level). Government public schools have a market share of 23 percent in urban areas and 17 percent in rural areas. Private schools are important in urban areas (28 percent market share), but rather limited in rural areas (less than 5 percent market share). Faith-based schools and public schools serve rather similar constituencies in regard to the level of well-being of the students as measured by the quintiles of per capita consumption. Private schools by contrast tend to serve on average better-off students, as expected.

In urban areas, faith-based schools have a large share of Catholic students (61 percent, versus overall market share of 51 percent), and they enroll relatively few children who do not belong to the main religions listed in the table (see table 8.2). However, as a rule, faith-based schools seem to be open to students from all backgrounds, and in rural areas especially, their student body seems roughly representative of the various faiths. This points to the fact that faith-based schools, which function in a way similar to public schools, do not discriminate against any specific religion.

To compare the performance of faith-based and government schools, we rely on two indicators: (1) whether students can read and write in French and (2) whether students are still enrolled in school between the ages of 13 and 18. Table 8.3 provides summary statistics on these two

Table 8.2   School Enrollment in Primary School by Student's Religion

	Catholic	Protestant	Other Christian	Other religion	Other	All
Urban						
Public	19.5	23.3	24.7	22.0	46.8	22.5
Religious	60.7	49.1	41.6	49.7	15.7	50.8
Private	19.7	27.5	33.7	28.3	37.5	26.7
All	100.0	100.0	100.0	100.0	100.0	100.0
Rural						
Public	17.9	13.1	21.4	13.8	22.4	16.5
Religious	78.1	83.6	68.7	82.7	71.7	78.7
Private	4.1	3.3	9.9	3.5	5.9	4.8
All	100.0	100.0	100.0	100.0	100.0	100.0
Congo, Dem. Rep. of						
Public	18.4	15.5	22.9	16.4	31.0	18.4
Religious	72.5	75.6	56.5	72.3	51.9	69.8
Private	9.1	8.9	20.6	11.3	17.1	11.8
All	100.0	100.0	100.0	100.0	100.0	100.0

Source: Authors' calculations using 1-2-3 survey, Democratic Republic of Congo, 2005.

Table 8.3   Performance Measurement by School Type

	% of students in primary schools who can read and write in French	% of students still enrolled in school at age 13–18 among those ever enrolled
Urban		
Public	24.4	60.4
Religious	24.7	71.6
Private	27.6	70.6
All	25.4	68.3
Rural		
Public	8.8	61.7
Religious	8.8	63.9
Private	12.2	74.4
All	9.0	64.0
Congo, Dem. Rep. of		
Public	14.9	61.2
Religious	12.5	65.2
Private	23.4	72.3
All	14.3	65.0

Source: Authors' calculations using 1-2-3 survey, Democratic Republic of Congo, 2005.

performance indicators among all children enrolled in school for the first indicator, and among all children 13–18 years of age for the second (for that indicator, we associate children who dropped out of school to various school networks on the basis of where the children went to school when they were still enrolled). Only a small minority of the students can read and write in French in primary schools. This is the case for 1 child in 4 in urban areas, and less than 1 child in 10 in rural areas. However, almost 2 in 3 children who previously enrolled in school are still enrolled in school at age 13–18.

Looking at the data at the national level in table 8.3, it is clear that students going to private schools tend to be better able to read and write, and they tend to have a higher probability of being enrolled at age 13–18. This is as expected given that these children come from slightly more privileged backgrounds. In regard to the comparison between government and faith-based schools, the ranking is less clear. On the one hand, a slightly higher proportion of students in government schools can read and write in French, but on the other hand, the proportion of children still enrolled at age 13–18 is higher in faith-based schools (this is however not necessarily a positive outcome because a higher enrollment rate may simply reflect more repetition).

For literacy, at least, much of the difference seems to be due to the geographic location of the schools. Faith-based schools are especially important in rural areas, where literacy is lower. If one looks at the average literacy rates in urban and rural areas separately, there are very few differences between public and faith-based schools. This illustrates how simple comparisons of performance between both types of schools may not account for the fact that there are potentially important differences in the types of students that enroll in government and faith-based schools. In the next section to assess performance controlling for a wide range of child and household characteristics and controlling for the possibility of endogenous school selection, we use regression techniques .

Econometric Analysis

Our technique for assessing the correlates of performance is simple and follows closely what was done for Sierra Leone by Wodon and Ying (2009). We estimate binary outcome (probit) models on whether or not a child can read or write, as well as whether the child is still enrolled at age 13–18, as a function of a large number of child, household, and geographic characteristics, including whether or not the child is in a faith-based or government school (children going to private schools are dropped from the sample). However, the choice of school for a child can itself depend on the child's performance. To avoid endogeneity bias, we instrument the choice of the type of school the child goes to through a first regression that includes as regressors all the correlates of the outcome regression, plus the leave-out share of the students in the child's geographic area that are going to faith-based schools (this follows among others Ravallion and Wodon 2000 and Wodon 2000). The child's geographic area is identified through the primary sampling unit to which the household belongs in the survey (each primary sampling unit includes typically between 20 and 30 households). We compute the leave-out participation rate in faith-based schools not taking into account whether the child himself or herself goes (thus, for each child in the same primary sampling unit, we compute a different leave-out mean; see Box 7.1 in Wodon and Ying [2009] in chapter 7 for a more detailed explanation of the method adopted).

The analysis is undertaken only on the sample of children who are attending government and faith-based schools. The regressors or correlates for the school choice and the performance of the student are (1) the type of school attended by the child (in the outcome regressions this variable is instrumented as explained above to avoid endogeneity issues); (2) the grade the child is in (first grade of the cycle is the reference category); (3) the time it takes for the child to go to school and the square of that time; (4) the characteristics of the child—the age of the child and the age squared, the gender of the child, whether the child lives with his or her parents; (5) the geographic location of the child according to urban or rural status and the main provinces in the country (we also run separate urban and rural regressions); (6) the quintile of per capita consumption of the household in which the child lives; (7) the religion of the child (with Catholic being the reference category); (8) household demographic variables—the household size and its square, whether the household head is male or female, and whether there is a spouse in the household; (9) the education level of the household head and spouse; and (10) the occupation of the father and the mother (farming is the reference category).

The first-stage regressions are not provided here but are available on request. They suggest that the religion of the child is not a key determinant of school choice, with two exceptions, in that "other Christian" children (i.e., those who are not Catholic or Protestant) and children whose parents declare not having a religion are less likely to go to faith-based schools. Another key result is that children from wealthier households are less likely to enroll in faith-based schools, although the effect is not systematic (remember that the sample is limited to children going to public and faith-based schools and does not include private school students). A better education for the household head and spouse makes it more likely that the child will go to a faith-based school, whereas a child in a female-headed household has a higher probability of going to a public school. Employment type for the household head or spouse in general does not have much impact on school choice, but the leave-out participation rate in faith-based schools, which is our instrument, is highly statistically significant, and the impact is also large, as expected.

We focus our discussion on the results of the outcome regressions, which are provided in table A8.1 and for literacy (for the probability of being still enrolled at age 13–18, the references are not shown as fewer variables are statistically significant, but the results are available upon request). The key variable of interest is the impact of the type of school attended by the child on performance as measured by literacy and the likelihood of still being enrolled at age 13–18. Controlling for other characteristics, attending a faith-based school increases literacy performance in the national-level regression (the effect is marginally significant at the 6 percent level), but not in the separate urban and rural regressions. The magnitude of the effect on literacy at the national level is also small. As for the probability of still being enrolled in school, the effect is not significant (even at the 10 percent level) either nationally or in the urban and rural regressions. Thus, one could argue that there are no substantial differences in performance between both sets of schools for either of the two outcome indicators.

A number of other results are worth noting. If a child is in a higher grade, the likelihood of being able to read or write a letter in English is higher, and this also increases the probability of being enrolled (for grades 3 to 5, but not for grade 6, as expected, because the child has then completed primary school). If children live with their parents, that has a positive effect on both literacy and the likelihood of being in school at age 13–18. The age of the child also increases the likelihood of literacy and enrollment. Girls are less likely to be literate than boys, and they are also less likely to be enrolled at age 13–18. Children from migrant households are more likely to be literate, but less likely to be enrolled at age 13–18. Religion does not seem to affect literacy and dropping out, controlling for other characteristics, but there are some geographic effects, with most provinces faring worse than the capital, Kinshasa. In most cases, the distance to schools does not affect literacy and dropout. By contrast, children from wealthier backgrounds are, as expected, more likely to be literate. Surprisingly, the education of the head or spouse does not have much impact on literacy or dropout, except when the head has a university-level education. The same is observed for the occupation of the head and spouse.

Conclusion

As a result of both historical factors and a legacy of conflict, faith-based schools account for 70 percent of students in primary schools in the Democratic Republic of Congo. Using a recent nationally representative and multipurpose household survey, the first such survey implemented in the country in more than 15 years, the objective of this chapter was to provide a comparative assessment of the performance of faith-based and government schools in regard to literacy (ability to read and write in French) and dropout (being enrolled in school at age 13–18).

Our results suggest that subjectively assessed literacy rates are very low in the Democratic Republic of Congo, which confirms previous research in this area. As expected, children who are better off tend to go to private schools instead of government or faith-based schools, and when they do go to government or faith-based schools, they tend to perform better (higher probability of literacy and lower probability of dropout). There are also differences between geographic areas in performance, but by contrast, differences related to the religion of the household, the education of the household head or spouse, and their occupation tend to be small.

In regard to the comparison of faith-based and public schools, simple basic statistics suggest few differences in outcomes measures between the two types of schools. The data also suggest that faith-based and government schools serve similar populations in regard to their levels of well-being. After controlling for child and household characteristics, and after taking into account the potential endogeneity of school choice depending on the performance of the student, we still find very few differences in performance between faith-based and public schools (all coefficients from the regression analysis are positive in favor of faith-based schools, but in most cases the coefficients are not statistically significant).

Our results do not suggest that in the Democratic Republic of Congo, faith-based schools provide better services than public schools. This result is different from those reported in the literature for other countries, in which faith-based schools tend to do slightly better than public schools. The fact that faith-based schools are comparable with public schools in the Democratic Republic of Congo could be related to the context of the country, whereby because of a lack of public financing, the cost of education essentially is borne by parents whether the children go to public or private schools. In addition, the very large market share of faith-based schools in the Democratic Republic of Congo makes it also more difficult to achieve excellence, or simply improve performance, across the board.

Annex: Regression Results

Table A8.1 Determinants of School Performance—Literacy

	National			Urban			Rural		
	Coef.	Std. err.	P>z	Coef.	Std. err.	P>z	Coef.	Std. err.	P>z
Religious school, instrumented	0.1574	0.0819	*	0.0886	0.1277	***	0.1530	0.1174	***
Grade									
Grade 1	réf								
Grade 2	0.1159	0.0642	*	0.1365	0.0833		0.0718	0.1089	
Grade 3	0.4117	0.0630	***	0.3401	0.0836	***	0.5242	0.1015	***
Grade 4	0.6365	0.0657	***	0.5590	0.0886	***	0.7632	0.1038	***
Grade 5	0.9569	0.0660	***	0.9035	0.0893	***	1.0601	0.1046	***
Grade 6	1.2903	0.1546	***	1.3113	0.1662	***	-4.7944	7497.4	
Child with biological parents	0.1049	0.0533	**	0.1101	0.0687		0.1315	0.0899	
Age	0.0372	0.0093	***	0.0283	0.0126	**	0.0495	0.0147	***
Age square	-0.0003	0.0002	**	-0.0002	0.0002		-0.0005	0.0003	**
Female (yes)	-0.1240	0.0355	***	-0.1120	0.0472	**	-0.1404	0.0563	**
Migrant (yes)	0.1131	0.0546	**	0.1704	0.0739	**	0.1407	0.0866	
Religion									
Catholic	réf								
Protestant	0.0229	0.0436		0.0642	0.0620		-0.0715	0.0648	
Kimbanguiste	-0.0907	0.1169		0.2481	0.1618		-0.4753	0.1919	**
Muslim	0.0183	0.1366		0.0439	0.1813		-0.1052	0.2203	
Other Christian	-0.0802	0.0529		-0.0776	0.0665		-0.1101	0.0950	
Animist	-0.2001	0.3337		-0.3556	0.4221		0.1033	0.5559	
Other religion	-0.0614	0.0773		-0.1102	0.1048		-0.0521	0.1208	
No religion	-0.0181	0.2127		0.2253	0.3769		-0.0795	0.2710	

	Coef.	SE	Sig.	Coef.	SE	Sig.	Coef.	SE	Sig.
Rural (yes)	−0.4285	0.0479	***						
Province									
Kinshasa	réf								
Bas-Congo	−0.3286	0.0890	***	−0.3055	0.1041	***	0.1100	0.1397	
Bandundu	−0.4487	0.0924	***	−0.3853	0.1119	***	−0.1186	0.1395	
Equateur	−0.5202	0.0892	***	−0.5694	0.1111	***	−0.1152	0.1268	
Orientale	−0.3770	0.0895	***	−0.4406	0.1118	***	0.1284	0.1309	
Nord-Kivu	−0.2372	0.0867	***	−0.1450	0.0982				
Maniema	−0.7391	0.0942	***	−0.7647	0.1214	***	−0.2309	0.1419	
Sud-Kivu	−0.4950	0.0918	***	−0.5509	0.1124	***	−0.0288	0.1348	
Katanga	−0.2065	0.0899	**	0.1190	0.1103		−0.1402	0.1384	
Kasai-Oriental	−0.3666	0.0939	***	−0.1101	0.1161		−0.1848	0.1567	
Kasai-Occidental	−0.7530	0.0968	***	−0.8024	0.1223	***	−0.2811	0.1549	*
Access to primary school									
Less than 1 km	réf								
1 km	0.0752	0.0567		0.1410	0.0801	*	0.0024	0.0853	
2–4 km	−0.0203	0.0684		−0.1724	0.1393		−0.0251	0.0829	
5–9 km	−0.0147	0.1125		0.2556	0.3784		−0.1511	0.1241	
10 km and more	−0.5453	0.3438		−4.7727	1017.0		−0.5770	0.3800	
Not available	0.1804	0.1021	*	0.3096	0.1488	**	−0.0229	0.1551	
Welfare									
Q1	réf								
Q2	0.0678	0.0545		0.0860	0.0757		0.0460	0.0823	
Q3	0.1189	0.0568	**	0.2569	0.0789	***	−0.0232	0.0874	
Q4	0.1296	0.0613	**	0.2357	0.0833	***	0.0108	0.0977	
Q5	0.3121	0.0695	***	0.4838	0.0939	***	0.0888	0.1147	

(continued)

Table A8.1 Determinants of School Performance—Literacy (Continued)

	National			Urban			Rural		
	Coef.	Std. err.	P>z	Coef.	Std. err.	P>z	Coef.	Std. err.	P>z
Household size	0.0041	0.0206		0.0354	0.0288		-0.0376	0.0316	
Household size square	0.0009	0.0009		-0.0003	0.0013		0.0023	0.0014	
Female head (yes)	0.1173	0.1101		0.2037	0.1382		0.0210	0.1889	
Spouse in the hh (yes)	0.2505	0.1603		0.2777	0.2043		0.2324	0.2834	
Education of the head									
No education	réf								
Primary	0.0632	0.0786		0.0289	0.1181		0.0697	0.1106	
Secondary	0.1088	0.0763		0.0981	0.1128		0.0923	0.1089	
Nonformal	0.2437	0.1705		0.3580	0.2052	*	-4.8995	892.2202	
University	0.1627	0.1051		0.1673	0.1381		-0.0055	0.2514	
Education of the spouse									
No education									
Primary	-0.0566	0.0569		-0.0834	0.0941		-0.0237	0.0752	
Secondary	0.0464	0.0594		0.0415	0.0922		0.0993	0.0854	
Nonformal	0.0486	0.2361		-0.0277	0.2602		-4.9249	1984.7	
University	0.4651	0.2093	**	0.5211	0.2343	**	-4.6740	2046.5	

	Coef.	S.E.		Coef.	S.E.		Coef.	S.E.	
Occupation of the head									
Wage earner, high level	réf								
Wage earner, others	-0.0545	0.0725		-0.0411	0.0842		-0.1049	0.1612	
Independent, nonagriculture	-0.1096	0.0648	*	-0.0706	0.0756		-0.1230	0.1494	
Independent, agriculture	-0.0952	0.0607		-0.0989	0.0838		-0.0621	0.1024	
Unpaid family worker	0.1104	0.0917		0.1032	0.1186		0.1381	0.1593	
Unemployed	-0.0858	0.0991		-0.1150	0.1120		0.3057	0.2358	
Inactive	0.0619	0.0915		0.0306	0.1098		0.0976	0.1822	
Occupation of the spouse									
Wage earner, high level	réf								
Wage earner, others	-0.1296	0.1752		-0.2766	0.2058		0.5416	0.3581	
Independent, nonagriculture	-0.1445	0.1217		-0.1162	0.1456		-0.4051	0.2809	
Independent, agriculture	-0.1823	0.1214		0.0312	0.1535		-0.3079	0.2212	
Unpaid family worker	-0.0905	0.1234		-0.1364	0.1641		-0.0972	0.2224	
Unemployed	-0.1070	0.1534		-0.0527	0.1769		-0.4816	0.4080	
Inactive	-0.2238	0.1222	*	-0.2858	0.1474	*	-0.0433	0.2398	
Constant	-1.8551	0.2077	***	-2.0585	0.2791	***	-2.4601	0.3269	***
Statistics									
Number of obs.	9505			4414			5091		
Wald chi2	1069.88			603.54			357.44		

Source: Authors' calculations using 1-2-3 survey, Democratic Republic of Congo, 2005.

References

Allcott, H., and D. E. Ortega. 2009. "The Performance of Decentralized School Systems: Evidence from Fe y Alegría in Venezuela." In *Emerging Evidence on Private Participation in Education: Vouchers and Faith-Based Providers*, ed. F. Barrera-Osorio, H. A. Patrinos, and Q. Wodon. Washington, DC: World Bank.

Altonji, J. G., T. E. Elder, and C. R. Taber. 2005. "An Evaluation of Instrumental Variable Strategies for Estimating the Effects of Catholic Schooling." *Journal of Human Resources* 40 (4): 791–821.

Asadullah, M. N., N. Chaudhury, and A. Dar. 2009. "Student Achievement in Religious and Secular Secondary Schools in Bangladesh." In *Emerging Evidence on Private Participation in Education: Vouchers and Faith-Based Providers*, ed. F. Barrera-Osorio, H. A. Patrinos, and Q. Wodon. Washington, DC: World Bank.

Bekalo, S., M. Brophy, and A. Welford. 2003. The Development of Education in Post-Conflict Somaliland." International *Journal of Educational Development* 23 (2): 459–75.

Cox, D,. and E. Jimenez. 1990. "The Relative Effectiveness of Private and Public Schools: Evidence from Two Developing Countries." *Journal of Development Economics* 34 (1–2) (November): 99–121.

Dennis, C., and A. Fentiman. 2007. "Alternative Basic Education in African Countries Emerging from Conflict: Issues of Policy, Co-ordination and Access." DFID Education Paper No. 67. Department for International Development, United Kingdom.

Evans, W., and R. Schwab. 1995. "Finishing High School and Starting College: Do Catholic Schools Make a Difference?" *Quarterly Journal of Economics* 110 (4) (November): 941–74.

González, R. A., and G. Arévalo. 2005. "Subsidized Catholic Schools in Venezuela." In *Private Education and Public Policy in Latin America*, ed. L. Wolff, J. C. Navarro, and P. González. Washington, DC: Project for Educational Revitalization in the Americas.

Hsieh, C., and M. Urquiola. 2006. "The Effects of Generalized School Choice on Achievement and Stratification: Evidence from Chile's School Voucher Program." *Journal of Public Economics* 90: 1477–1503.

Hoxby, C. M. 1994. "Do Private Schools Provide Competition for Public Schools?" NBER (National Bureau of Economic Research) Working Paper 4978. NBER, Cambridge, MA.

Ravallion M., and Q. Wodon. 2000. "Does Child Labor Displace Schooling? Evidence on Behavioral Responses to an Enrollment Subsidy." *Economic Journal* 110: C158–75.

Reinikka, R., and J. Svensson. Forthcoming. "Working for God? Evidence from a Change in Financing of Not-for-Profit Health Care Providers in Uganda." *Journal of the European Economic Association.*

Wodon Q. 2000. "Low Income Energy Assistance and Disconnection in France." *Applied Economics Letters* 7: 775–79.

Wodon, Q., and Y. Ying. 2009. "Literacy and Numeracy in Faith-Based and Government Schools in Sierra Leone." In *Emerging Evidence on Private Participation in Education: Vouchers and Faith-Based Providers*, ed. F. Barrera-Osorio, H. A. Patrinos, and Q. Wodon. Washington, DC: World Bank.

World Bank. 2005. "Education in the Democratic Republic of Congo: Priorities and Options for Regeneration." World Bank Country Studies, Washington, DC.

———. 2008. "Democratic Republic of Congo: Poverty Diagnostic." Report No. 36489-Democratic Republic of Congo. World Bank, Washington, DC.

CHAPTER 9

Assessing the Performance of Madrasas in Rural Bangladesh

Mohammad Niaz Asadullah, Nazmul Chaudhury, and Amit Dar

Introduction

The objective of this chapter is to compare the performance of Islamic (madrasa) secondary schools and secular secondary schools in rural Bangladesh.[1] Previous work on relative quality of madrasa education was conducted in Indonesia by Beegle and Newhouse (2005), who find that students attending public madrasas perform no worse than those attending public secular schools, and students attending private madrasas perform no worse than their counterparts in private secular schools. In this chapter, we assess the quality of religious and secular education in rural Bangladesh using a unique, large-scale survey of secondary schools. Quality is measured on the basis of the performance of students in mathematics, collected using two standardized tests.

The pretertiary education sector in Bangladesh has a complex structure in which the composition of the sector changes as one moves from primary (grades 1 to 5) to secondary (grades 6 to 10) levels. At the primary level, there are various service providers; however, the majority of schools are government operated (or financed). This sector also contains a significant number of NGO-run nonformal schools, with a rising share of private schools as well. The share of madrasa education in the primary sector is extremely small, even in rural areas. That is, however, not the case in the secondary sector, in which the dominant mode of service delivery combines public financing with private delivery. Hence, although there are only a few government-run secondary schools (most located in urban areas and district headquarters), more than 95 percent of secondary schools are operated by the private sector with government financing. In the private sector, the share of madrasas is significant.

Bangladesh has been one of the most ambitious countries in attempting to reform the madrasa (Islamic) school system at the secondary level. First, it introduced fiscal incentives to orthodox unregistered all-male madrasas high schools to register and include modern subjects such as physics and mathematics. Then it introduced another financial incentive to registered madrasa high schools to start admitting female students. Most madrasa secondary schools are now registered and follow a modern curriculum alongside traditional religious subjects. However, the most remarkable aspect of these secondary schools is that they have become coed (50 percent of the enrollment in madrasa high schools now consists of females)—an unparalleled development in South Asia so far.

Given that almost 100 percent of teacher salary is covered by the government in both secular and madrasa public-aided secondary schools, the teacher incentive regime in rural areas does not vary much across school type. These recognized madrasas are comparable with private schools for another reason. They offer a modern curriculum in which, alongside religious subjects, students are educated in mathematics, science, English, and geography. On completion of grade 10, students take the SSC examination, which is organized separately by the Madrasa Education Board. Graduates of madrasas are eligible for admission to mainstream education institutes for higher education. They also compete with their secular-schooled peers for employment in the public sector.[2]

Reliable data on the performance of Bangladeshi students in internationally comparable scholastic tests are not available. Bangladesh has not participated in international tests. Locally administered tests of students on secondary school achievement are almost nonexistent. Nonetheless, it is possible to assess the quality of secondary schooling indirectly by looking at the performance of secondary school students in primary standard tests. Greaney et al. (1999) did a comprehensive study in which they developed a basic test of learning skills in reading, writing, written mathematics, and oral mathematics and in 1992 administered it to a sample of 5,235 individuals, 11 years old or older, in 29 rural subdistricts *(thanas)*. The authors found that 59 percent of rural children correctly performed only five or fewer of eight tasks requiring the recognition of one- and two-digit numbers, the writing of one-digit numbers, and the recognition of basic geometric shapes. The figure was somewhat larger for primary school graduates who had completed some secondary schooling. Even then, 20 percent of the grade 8 completers failed to attain basic competency in mathematics. Given the rudimentary nature of the test items, this finding suggests that the level of school quality in rural Bangladesh is very low.

In the absence of individual-level test score data on secondary schools, other studies have either used data on school-level performance in public examination or analyzed labor market performance of graduates of different school types. For instance, Asadullah (2005a) uses school-level data on SSC pass rates on all secondary private, aided, and public schools in seven districts in Bangladesh and explores the role of class size on examination performance. However, the study precludes religious schools. Two studies that shed some light on the relative quality of religious schools are Asadullah (2005b) and Asadullah (2006). These papers document labor market returns to education by school type and report moderate wage disadvantage experienced by religious school graduates.

The relative performance of religious and secular schools aside, another aspect of the current debate over secondary school quality involves gender differences in achievement. This is owing to the existence of gender-specific incentive schemes that today cover all rural and non-metropolitan urban areas of Bangladesh. Female students of both religious and secular (recognized) schools in rural and urban nonmetropolitan areas benefit from a government subsidy scheme, also known as the Female Stipend Program (FSP). Since its initiation in 1994, Bangladesh has seen a steady rise in female enrollment in rural areas. Under the project, girls in grades 6 to 10 receive monthly stipends that cover the direct costs of schooling. The program has also increased the number of female teachers in rural schools. In sum, the stipend program has succeeded in changing the gender pattern of enrollment and composition of teachers in schools.

The structural changes in the secondary education sector brought about by the stipend scheme are evident. Today, 6.5 percent to 20 percent of school teachers are female, and there is (over) parity in female enrollment at the secondary level. Girls are more likely to enroll in school and complete higher grades compared with boys. Given the shortage of public schools for the provision of secondary education in the rural areas, the government has included recognized religious schools in the stipend scheme. Consequently, half the total enrollment in religious schools today also is composed of female students. The program has led to a large-scale expansion of religious schools in the rural areas. Yet, the quality of these secondary schools has so far remained out of the policy debate, primarily because of a lack of data on secondary school learning outcomes. A study on secondary schools not only can fill in the gap on information about the quality of religious and secular schools in rural areas, but it can also provide information about the relative performance of boys compared with girls.

To compare the performance of various types of schools, it is necessary to take into account the endogeneity of school selection. In Bangladesh, despite adoption of a modern curriculum and public funding, religious schools differ from secular schools. For example, they explicitly emphasize the importance of religious values and discipline in life. Ideally, one should exploit an experimental or quasi-experimental setting that gives rise to exogenous variation in education inputs. This has been attempted in a number of recent studies (Case and Deaton 1999; Angrist and Lavy 1999). Often, nonetheless, even quasi-experimental settings akin to Angrist and Lavy (1999) are rare. Consequently, careful design of the sample to circumvent the problem of identification is the way forward.

To deal with the issue of endogeneity, a variety of instruments have been constructed in the literature using either demand- or supply-side information. The former relates to exogenous personal attributes that are correlated with preference for a particular school type yet arguably uncorrelated with learning outcomes. The supply-side-related instruments usually exploit information on the availability of a given school type and attributes of schools available in one's residential vicinity. Developing country studies by Beegle and Newhouse (2005), Alderman et al. (2001), Glewwe et al. (1995), and Glewwe and Jacoby (1994) have adopted the second strategy. The last three are intuitively more appealing because they use characteristics of the school not chosen as the identifying variables, instead of data on the availability of a given school type.

A richer set of instruments using demand-side information has been used in developed country literature. In analyses of the influence of Catholic schooling on learning outcomes, U.S. researchers used as instruments the religious beliefs of the student's family (Evans and Schwab 1995; Neal 1997), proportion of Catholics in the area, proximity of Catholic schooling, urbanity (Evans and Schwab 1995; Neal 1997), and interactions between religious beliefs and urbanity (Sander 1996). More recently Figlio and Stone (2000) have used variables such as the crime rate in the county, concentration of the public schools in the county (i.e., public school student-to-teacher ratios), and community characteristics to model selection into a given school type.

In this chapter we follow Alderman et al. (2001) in using information on the quality of unchosen schools in administrative neighborhoods to construct instruments. In addition, drawing on the U.S. studies, we use measures of parental religiosity as an additional instrument. The structure of the chapter is as follows. The next section discusses the data and provides summary statistics. A section presenting the results of econometric estimations follows, and a brief conclusion ends the chapter.

Data and Summary Statistics

The data were collected to assess school quality in rural Bangladesh within the context of the Female Secondary School Assistance Project (FSSAP) jointly initiated by the World Bank and the government of Bangladesh in 1993. This is one of the four stipend schemes and today covers more than 5,000 secondary education institutes in a total of 118 thanas and 1,063 unions. A simple clustered sampling procedure was used to select schools for the survey. All recognized schools and madrasas in each selected union were surveyed. In total, 321 schools and madrasas could be identified in 60 unions or school catchment areas. The survey was conducted in 2005.

Two mathematics tests were administered to all students (both boys and girls) enrolled in grade 8 and present on the day of the survey, irrespective of whether an individual student was on stipend or not. The first test was based on secondary standard mathematics knowledge. The test instrument was constructed by using items previously used in the Trends in International Mathematics and Science Study (TIMSS), 1999. The TIMSS has been administered three times by the International Association for the Evaluation of Educational Achievement (IEA), the latest in 2003. The study has released several secondary standard (grade 8) mathematics items indicating what each item measures and the results of every participating country. The TIMSS instrument assessed competency in data, measurement, number, algebra, and geometry using 125 multiple-choice format mathematics items.[3] On the basis of pilot test experience and given the time constraint in the field, only 20 original items were retained in our test instrument. These included 9 questions on numbers and fractions, 3 on geometry, 6 on algebra, 1 on graphs, and 1 on measurement. The second test instrument is based on the primary school mathematics syllabus. This test assessed students using four very basic free-response format questions that were used by Greaney et al. (1999)

to assess competency in written mathematics among primary school graduates in Bangladesh in 1992.

For each school, the head teacher was interviewed to gather data on various aspects of the school and the average background of the teachers. If the head teacher was absent, the teacher-in-charge was interviewed. In addition, school registers were accessed to collect data on student performance in the school final examination in grade 7 in the previous year. This way, retrospectively, we collected data on seventh grade final math, English, and total test scores for all sample students. In addition to test scores, the survey collected data on a host of school and teacher characteristics. All students taking the test were asked to answer a number of questions relating to their families and parental background. Detailed data on personal characteristics and the history of presecondary schooling (such as types of primary and preprimary school attended) were also collected. Family-related information on sample students was collected without any household visits. Last, in addition to test score data on all schools in the sample, we collected data for a subsample of 34 schools (10 percent of the original sample); the primary standard mathematics test was administered to all students enrolled in grade 6.

All students in grade 8 were given a test based on four simple questions that assessed basic numeracy skills requiring the knowledge of primary-level mathematics. These questions were used by Greaney et al. (1999) to assess basic competency in mathematics in rural Bangladesh. Depending on the question, failure rate ranged from 14 percent to 40 percent for girls, whereas the range was much narrower for boys, that is, 10 percent to 28 percent. The mean total score (correct answers) stands at only 77 percent (3.10 of 4). Greaney et al. defined competency in rudimentary-level mathematics in terms of ability to correctly answer at least three of the questions in each set. Therefore, we calculated the fraction of students who were able to answer at least three questions correctly. That yields figures that are comparable with those reported in Greaney et al. (1999). Only 75 percent of students could attain basic competency in written mathematics despite the fact that the test instrument used to assess competency was based on the primary-school mathematics curriculum. This figure is consistent with the competency level among grade 7 and 8 completers reported by Greaney et al., that is, 60 percent and 80 percent, respectively. Thus one could conclude that the level of competency has not improved much during the decade.

Table 9.1 summarizes mean aggregate scores of grade 6 and 8 students. Two patterns emerge. First, mean percentage of correct answers among

Table 9.1   Mean Correct Scores in Primary Math Test by School Type, Grade, and Gender

		Full sample	Other schools	Madrasa
Grade 6 math score	Full	0.42	0.42	0.45
	Males	0.54	0.57	0.52
	Females	0.35	0.36	0.34
Grade 8 math score	Full	0.57	0.57	0.57
	Males	0.66	0.66	0.67
	Females	0.50	0.50	0.51

Source: Authors' estimations.
Note: Figures show the fraction of answers that are correct.

grade 6 students remains abysmally low. On average, students could answer only 42 percent of the test questions correctly. When grade 8 students of the same school were asked to answer the same questions, the mean score went up, but only moderately (by 15 percentage points). It seems that although the quality of secondary education remains low (in regard to insufficient value addition), much of it might have to do with the poor quality of education received in rural primary schools in Bangladesh.

The differences in test scores between madrasas and other schools are not significant. However, there are differences by gender. Boys still have higher scores than girls in grades 6 and 8. To be precise, the gender gap in test scores exists at the beginning of secondary education and prevails through grade 8.

Regression Results

Our econometric methodology is described in detail in Asadullah et al. (forthcoming). As instruments for religious school attendance, we use data on parental religiosity and relative characteristics of secular schools in the catchment area of the schools. Results of a number of different econometric specifications are discussed in Asadullah et al. (forthcoming). Here, we focus directly in Table A9.1 on the key results from the likely better specification.

Column 1 provides estimations with school fixed effects (FEs). Primary education in an NGO school has a significant negative effect on secondary school test scores. Being educated in a primary madrasa has a negative effect, which is significant at the conventional level. Preprimary schooling has a small negative effect. Class rank in the previous grade final examination continues to exert a significant effect: students who academically ranked low among their peers in the previous grade perform poorly compared with those with superior ranking. Female students have lower test scores compared with male peers. Class size still has a perverse positive and significant effect. This result is counterintuitive but consistent with other studies on class size (Asadullah 2005a, 2005b; Wößmann and West 2002). Column 2 reports estimates with classroom fixed effects. The estimated impact of gender and primary school types is similar to that obtained in column 1. The only difference relates to the fact that the positive effect of having primary education in the current (secondary) school is now statistically significant.

Conclusion

Several important findings emanate from this study. First, on average, school quality measured by test performance is very low in rural Bangladesh. Only 14 percent of students could correctly answer 60 percent of the secondary-level mathematics test questions. Second, we find that girls have a lower test score than boys, controlling for various school and background factors. Third, school choice matters—children who attend religious schools are worse off compared with their secular-schooled peers. However, once the decision to attend a religious school is treated as endogenous, no significant difference in test scores prevails between religious and secular school students. Madrasa attendance for primary education, however, exerts a significant negative effect on test scores even after accounting for school-specific unobservable determinants of learning. Fourth, our evidence does not support the view that reducing class size boosts learning outcomes. Finally, a gender difference in test scores persists even after controlling for stipend status and all school- and classroom-specific unobserved factors. This learning disadvantage of the girls is puzzling considering that for many girls there are financial incentives to improve performance. Female students all over rural Bangladesh benefit from the FSP, which conditions stipend payment on a minimum achievement in school-level examinations and regular attendance in school. No such learning incentives (in financial terms) exist for boys.

School choice studied in this chapter has not accounted for the option of nonformal religious education in the rural area. Although the share of enrollment in traditional madrasa schools is very small, it is still important to document the extent and quality of these schools. A large number of traditional madrasas in Bangladesh and elsewhere in South Asia follow orthodox curricula, which educate children exclusively in religious matters. It remains to be seen how parental decision to choose modern religious schooling over secular education is affected when they have access to traditional religious schools. Future studies on religious schools should distinguish between modern and traditional types and assess their competitive position in relation to other nonfaith schools. Given that the traditional faith schools do not impart any skills that are relevant for a modern economy, knowledge of how student selection into these schools is affected by the presence of modern religious and secular schools will have important added value for future policy reforms.

Annex: Regression Results

Table A9.1   Determinants of Student Achievement
(percentage of correct answers in math test)

	School FE	Classroom FE
Student attributes		
Age	−0.003	−0.003
	(0.62)	(0.60)
Age squared	0.000	0.000
	(0.14)	(0.10)
Non Muslim	−0.002	−0.002
	(0.29)	(0.39)
Female	−0.025	−0.025
	(4.84)**	(4.73)**
Female* (girl currently on stipend)	0.008	0.008
	(1.48)	(1.51)
Family background		
Father primary educated	−0.003	−0.003
	(0.66)	(0.74)
Father secondary educated	0.005	0.005
	(1.11)	(1.14)
Father higher educated	0.013	0.014
	(2.89)**	(3.00)**
Mother primary educated	0.008	0.008
	(2.38)*	(2.34)*
Mother secondary educated	0.009	0.009
	(2.09)*	(2.20)*
Mother higher educated	0.016	0.015
	(2.80)**	(2.70)**
Household has a mobile phone	0.009	0.009
	(2.33)*	(2.39)*
House being pucca	0.001	0.002
	(0.22)	(0.45)
House being semi-pucca	0.002	0.003
	(0.59)	(0.71)
Travel time to school from home	−0.000	−0.000
	(1.49)	(1.22)
Schooling history		
Had preprimary (maktab) education in childhood	−0.001	−0.001
	(12.68)**	(12.19)**
Class rank in grade 7	−0.012	−0.012
	(3.01)**	(3.13)**
Attended primary private school	−0.012	−0.011
	(1.49)	(1.43)
Attended primary madrasa	−0.014	−0.013
	(2.05)*	(2.00)*

(continued)

Table A9.1   Determinants of Student Achievement *(Continued)*

(percentage of correct answers in math test)

	School FE	Classroom FE
Attended primary NGO school	−0.007	−0.007
	(0.71)	(0.70)
Attended primary grade in this school	0.005	0.007
	(1.47)	(2.00)*
Secondary school attributes		
Class size	0.001	
	(4.11)**	
N	7482	7482
Number of FEs	298	320
Adjusted R²	0.04	0.04

Source: Authors' estimations.

Note: Absolute value of *t* statistics in parentheses.

+ significant at 10%.

* significant at 5%.

** significant at 1 percent. Each regression in addition contains a set of five dummies indicating which day of the week the test was taken.

Notes

1. This chapter summarizes a forthcoming paper by the authors in *Education Economics* titled "School Choice and Cognitive Achievement in Rural Bangladesh." We are grateful to Quentin Wodon of the World Bank's Development Dialogue for Values and Ethics for drafting the summary from the original paper.

2. For a comprehensive review of the madrasa education system in Bangladesh, see Asadullah et al. (2006).

3. It also contained 37 free-response format questions that were not considered while our test instrument was being designed. See Garden and Smith (2000) for details.

References

Alderman, H., P. F. Orazem, and E. M. Paterno. 2001. "School Quality, School Cost, and the Public/Private School Choices of Low-Income Households in Pakistan." *Journal of Human Resources* 36: 304–26.

Angrist, J., and V. Lavy. 1999. "Using Maimonides' Rule to Estimate the Effect of Class Size on Children's Academic Achievement." *Quarterly Journal of Economics* 114 (2): 533–76.

Asadullah, M. N. 2005a. "The Effect of Class Size on Student Achievement: Evidence from Bangladesh." *Applied Economics Letters* 12 (4): 217–21.

————. 2005b. "The Effectiveness of Private and Public Schools in Bangladesh and Pakistan." Paper presented at the Global Conference on Education Research in Developing Countries, Prague, Czech Republic, March 31–April 2.

————. 2006. "Returns to Education in Bangladesh." *Education Economics* 14 (4): 453–68.

Asadullah, M., N., N. Chaudhury, and A. Dar. Forthcoming. "Student Achievement Conditioned Upon School Selection: Religious and Secular Secondary School Quality in Bangladesh." *Education Economics.*

Beegle, C., and D. Newhouse. 2005. "The Effect of School Type on Academic Achievement: Evidence from Indonesia." Policy Research Working Papers. World Bank, Washington, DC.

Case, A., and A. Deaton. 1999. "School Inputs and Educational Outcomes In South Africa." *Quarterly Journal of Economics* 11 4(3): 1047–84.

Figlio, D. N. and J. Stone. 2000. "Are Private Schools Really Better?" *Research in Labor Economics* 18: 115–40.

Garden, R. A., and T. A. Smith. 2000. "TIMSS Test Development." In *TIMSS 1999 Technical Report*, ed. M. O. Martin, K. D. Gregory, and S. E. Stemler. Chestnut Hill, MA: Boston College.

Glewwe, P., and H. Jacoby. 1994. "Student Achievement and Schooling Choice in Low-Income Countries: Evidence from Ghana." *Journal of Human Resources* 29 (3): 843–64.

Glewwe, P., M. Grosh, H. Jacoby, and M. Lockheed. 1995. "An Eclectic Approach to Estimating the Determinants of Achievement in Jamaican Primary Education." *World Bank Economic Review* 9 (2): 231–58.

Greaney, V., S. R. Khandker, and M. Alam. 1999. Bangladesh: Assessing Basic Learning Skills. Dhaka, Bangladesh: University Press.

Jepsen, C. 2003. "The Effectiveness of Catholic Primary Schooling." *Journal of Human Resources* 38 (4): 928.

Neal, D. 1997. "The Effects of Catholic Secondary Schooling on Educational Attainment." *Journal of Labor Economics* 15: 98–123.

Sander, W. 1996. "Catholic Grade Schools and Academic Achievement." *Journal of Human Resources* 31 (3): 540–48.

Wößmann, L., and M. R. West. 2002. "Class-Size Effects in School Systems Around the World: Evidence from Between-Grade Variation in TIMSS." Kiel Institute of World Economics Working Paper No. 1099.

PART III

Private Cost of Education

CHAPTER 10

Does Money Matter? The Effect of Private Education Expenditures on Academic Performance in the Republic of Korea

Changhui Kang

Introduction

The causal relationship between education investments and student outcomes continues to attract the attention of many. Despite decades of intensive study, there is no consensus on the effectiveness of monetary education inputs for student outcomes. On one hand, papers that summarize the debate on the effects of public school expenditures often advocate conflicting views (Betts 1996; Card and Krueger 1996; Hanushek 2003). On the other, studies focusing on private schools (e.g., Catholic schools) do not provide much insight on the impacts of education expenditures (Altonji et al. 2005).

In this chapter we attempt to shed light on the effectiveness of education investments by examining private education expenditures. Specifically, we look into academic effects of the expenditures on private tutoring services, which are widely used by parents in the Republic of Korea to supplement public school education.

In Korea, secondary school students have little freedom in the choice of their middle and high schools in their school districts. Since 1969 student allocation to public and private schools has largely been under the strict control of the government, especially in urban regions. Under this system (labeled Leveling Policy), students are basically assigned—not admitted upon application—to secondary schools in their residential school district by either a pure lottery or an application-accompanied-by-lottery system under the supervision of the local Ministry of Education office. Moreover, within schools, ability grouping is rarely implemented as a result of the government's egalitarian policy on secondary education and parents' objections. Curricula are also controlled for the most part by the Ministry of Education.

In response to such a rigid public education system, parents in Korea spend a significant amount of money on private tutoring for their children. According to statistics, Korean parents spend 85 percent as much on private tutoring as they spend on public schooling (KEDI [Korean Educational Development Institute] 1998). Given such large expenditures on private tutoring, many, including parents and education policy makers, are concerned about the effectiveness of private tutoring on student academic performance. From a broader perspective, an examination of the effect of private tutoring serves to illuminate the debates on the impacts of education inputs on student outcomes.

It is well known that education expenditures are not exogenously and randomly determined; there is little doubt that private tutoring expenditures are endogenous and correlated with a student's personal, family, and academic characteristics. In the absence of a randomized experiment on private tutoring, a causal estimation calls for a variable that strongly affects the parents' decision to invest in a child's education, but is independent of education outcomes (academic performance among others) when tutoring expenditures are controlled for. For such a variable this chapter uses a student's birth order in the family. A large body of literature theoretically and empirically documents that parents favor a certain-parity child (e.g., first-born or last-born) in education. As long as a student's birth order is exogenously determined by how many older siblings were born before him or her, however, it is unlikely to affect the academic performance of the student.[1]

Using a student's birth order as an instrumental variable (IV), this chapter shows that a 10 percent increase in private education expenditure leads to a 0.56 percentile point improvement in test scores.[2] Evaluated at the mean value, this amount of effect is equivalent to a 1.1 percent increase in test score due to a 10 percent increase in expenditure. Our estimated effect of private education expenditures is modest and fairly comparable with the effect of public school expenditures on earnings estimated by previous studies (e.g., Card and Krueger 1996).

The rest of the chapter is organized as follows. A description of private tutoring in Korea is presented in the next section, followed by a section with a discussion of the data. The empirical strategy is discussed in the subsequent section, followed by a section presenting the empirical results. A concluding section ends the chapter.

Private Tutoring in Korea

There are many forms of private tutoring that a student may receive for various reasons. The tutoring varies from a swimming lesson for exercise to math tutoring for a slow-learning child. Here we focus on a private supplementary instruction of academic subjects that involves financial transactions outside the formal school system. Such private tutoring is generally observed in many countries in which the public education system is poorly equipped or the existing system fails to satisfy highly motivated parents. Although it is apparently most prominent in East Asian societies such as Japan, Hong Kong, Taiwan, and Korea (*Time Asia* 2006), studies report private tutoring in a wide range of countries from Egypt, Kenya, India, Romania, Canada, and the United Kingdom (Baker et al. 2001; Bray 1999).

In Korea there exist widespread and large-scale markets for private tutoring outside the public education system, with quite large private tutoring expenditures by parents. The Ministry of Education (1999, 2000) shows that, for all income groups, private tutoring expenses are about 9 percent of total income for households with school-age children. At the national level, total household expenditures on private tutoring in 2003 amount to 2.3 percent of the national GDP and 55 percent of the national annual budget for public education (Korean Educational Development Institute, *Media Briefing*, November 19, 2003). A major reason for such widespread private tutoring in the country is that there are virtually no private secondary schools that are independent of the government's control. In Korea, private middle and high schools are little different from public schools with respect to school administration, curriculum, and student placement because they are heavily subsidized and controlled by the government.[3]

Among potentially many channels of private instruction, only two broad types of private tutoring are permitted by the government and practiced in the market in Korea. One is a relatively formal instruction offered by *hakwons*, private, for-profit school-like learning institutions. The other is an informal private instruction by individual university students. All other forms of private tutoring, including private instruction by full-time school teachers outside the school or by *hakwon* instructors outside the *hakwon* as well as private tutoring through the mail, by phone, or using TVs, are prohibited by the government. Of the two legal forms of private tutoring, the government maintains a strong control over *hakwons*, although it has little control over individual tutors. The government imposes some requirements for establishing a *hakwon* and exerts administrative controls with respect to pricing, academic qualification of tutors, physical facilities, and so on (Kim and Lee 2001).

According to our data from the Korean Education and Employment Panel (discussed shortly), the proportion of grade 11 students who receive private tutoring for any subject is 77.8 percent, and their overall average monthly spending on private tutoring is about W285,400 or approximately US$239, which amounts to 9 percent of monthly family income (see table 10.1). Among academic subjects, private tutoring is most frequently practiced for mathematics (51.8 percent). Of those students who receive private tutoring for math, 45.4 percent use *hakwons* and 47.4 percent use one-to-one or one-to-many tutoring offered by individual tutors.

Data

For the empirical analysis this study employs the Korean Education and Employment Panel (KEEP). KEEP is a longitudinal study that has been conducted since 2004 by the Korea Research Institute for Vocational Education and Training (KRIVET), a government-funded research institute. The basic structure of KEEP follows the National Educational Longitudinal Studies (NELS) of the United States. The beginning cohorts of KEEP consist of 6,000 students from three different populations: 2,000 students each from middle school (grade 9), general high school (grade 12, the final year of secondary education), and vocational high school (grade 12, the final year of secondary education). Students of each group are sampled by the stratification method to reflect the national population of the group. More specifically, for each group 100 schools are selected in consideration of the regional distribution of schools and students. For each school four different classes are randomly chosen, and for each class five students are sampled at random. The sampled students are administered a variety of personal, family, and

Table 10.1 Descriptive Statistics of the Main Sample

		Total sample		(1) First-borns		(2) Later-borns		Differences [(1)–(2)]		
Variable	N	Mean	S.D.	Mean	S.D.	Mean	S.D.	Mean	S.D.	T-value
Take test (No=1)	1752	0.134	0.341	0.135	0.342	0.133	0.339	0.003	0.016	0.17
Average score of three tests	1503	49.00	22.68	50.65	22.36	47.07	22.9	3.571	1.170	3.05
Test score of Korea	1490	49.75	25.82	51.72	25.59	47.42	25.93	4.302	1.338	3.21
Test score of mat	1419	48.97	26.33	49.22	26.31	48.67	26.36	0.549	1.404	0.39
Test score of English	1490	49.37	26.21	51.77	25.86	46.57	26.37	5.195	1.356	3.83
Tutoring expenditure (W1,000)	1749	285.4	341.1	323.8	375.6	240.5	289.6	83.31	16.25	5.13
Any tutoring (Yes=1	1749	0.778	0.416	0.830	0.376	0.716	0.451	0.114	0.020	5.79
Tutoring hours for Korea	1752	1.295	2.504	1.448	2.607	1.116	2.368	0.331	0.120	2.76
Tutoring for Korean (Yes=1)	1752	0.301	0.459	0.338	0.473	0.258	0.438	0.080	0.022	3.64
Tutoring hours for math	1752	2.464	3.136	2.746	3.251	2.134	2.963	0.612	0.150	4.09
Tutoring for math (Yes=1)	1752	0.518	0.500	0.576	0.495	0.451	0.498	0.125	0.024	5.24
Tutoring hours for English	1752	1.732	2.627	1.956	2.520	1.471	2.725	0.485	0.125	3.86
Tutoring for English (Yes=1)	1752	0.410	0.492	0.473	0.500	0.337	0.473	0.136	0.023	5.82
Prior quality	1285	46.12	26.68	45.13	26.18	47.30	27.23	-2.169	1.493	-1.45
Hours of self-study	1752	11.34	10.22	11.62	10.35	11.01	10.06	0.613	0.490	1.25
Age	1752	17.74	0.517	17.72	0.521	17.75	0.512	-0.026	0.025	-1.05
Male (Yes=1)	1752	0.580	0.494	0.577	0.494	0.585	0.493	-0.008	0.024	-0.34
Only child (Yes=1)	1752	0.075	0.263	0.139	0.346	0.000	0.000	0.139	0.012	11.39
Number of siblings	1752	2.192	0.663	1.997	0.540	2.420	0.719	-0.423	0.030	-14.05
Parents' average age	1751	46.06	3.178	44.91	2.816	47.40	3.050	-2.493	0.140	-17.78
Parents' average education	1748	12.10	2.538	12.46	2.471	11.68	2.553	0.781	0.120	6.48
Both parents present (Yes=1)	1752	0.922	0.269	0.921	0.270	0.923	0.266	-0.003	0.013	-0.20
Single father (Yes=1)	1752	0.027	0.162	0.030	0.170	0.024	0.152	0.006	0.008	0.79
Single mother (Yes=1)	1752	0.051	0.221	0.050	0.218	0.053	0.225	-0.004	0.011	-0.34
Books at home	1752	184.1	211.3	196.0	217.3	170.2	203.2	25.75	10.11	2.55
Family income (W1,000)	1730	318.8	196.7	332.4	200.9	302.9	190.6	29.47	9.465	3.11
First-born child (Yes=1)	1752	0.539	0.499							

Source: Author's calculations.

155

school-related questionnaires; and teachers, school principals, and parents are separately surveyed to collect background information.

An important feature of the KEEP data is that the survey collects detailed information on a student's private tutoring experience and expenditures and the sibling composition from the parent question-naire, which enables us to construct explanatory and instrumental variables for this study. Also unique in the KEEP data is the availability of the College Scholastic Ability Test (CSAT) scores for high school graduates. CSAT is the national college entrance examination in Korea, which is annually administered under the supervision of the Ministry of Education and whose scores are used by colleges and universities as an important factor in making admission decisions. Using the resident registration number of the student, the KEEP data are linked to the administrative database of the 2004 CSAT scores for the test writers. As a measure of a student's academic performance, we use the CSAT score percentiles of the following three subjects: the Korean language, mathematics, and English. The score percentile of each individual subject ranges from 0 (lowest score) to 100 (highest score). Given the percentile score of each subject, the average of the three individual percentiles is calculated and used for our main analysis.

Although vocational high school graduates are eligible for CSAT, the majority of the CSAT takers are general high school graduates, who are also the majority among students using private tutoring. Therefore, we restrict our analysis to the general high school sample of 2,000 students.[4]

For the analysis, some observations were dropped from the original sample. First, we exclude those students whose guardian is not one of the parents, since patterns of private education investment and academic performance among these students may be far from typical because of the absence of at least one parent. Second, we exclude students attending a special high school for music, fine arts, and athletics and those using private tutoring to major in these subjects for higher education in universities, because tutoring costs among these students are generally much greater than costs of tutoring on academic subjects.[5] The final sample has 1,752 students. Descriptive statistics of the main sample and the differences between first-born and later-born students are documented in table 10.1.

Among CSAT takers, the mean score percentile in Korean is 49.8; the mean score percentiles for math and English are 49.0 and 49.4, respectively. Although mean math percentiles are similar between the two groups, mean percentiles for Korean and English among first-born significantly exceed those of later-born students. Mean score percentiles averaged over the three subjects are also significantly greater for first-born than for later-born students. Yet it is not clear whether these differences between the two groups are determined by birth order or created by contemporary variations in education investment.

As for the amount of spending on private tutoring, first-born students receive larger education investments from their parents than later-born counterparts do.[6] While the overall average monthly spending on private tutoring is about W285,400, approximately $239, the average spending for first-born students (W323,800) is 35 percent greater than that for later-borns (W240,500). This gap is significantly different from zero. The proportion of those who have received private tutoring at least once—those with positive monthly spending—is also higher among first-born students (83.0 percent) than among later-born (71.6 percent) students. Namely, first-born students seem to receive significantly greater education investments than later-born ones do.

Empirical Framework

For our empirical analysis we consider a value-added model of education production. We estimate a regression of the average percentile test score of students versus the monthly spending on tutoring, the pretutorial performance of the student at grade 11, and a set of personal, family, and school characteristics. To account for problems of endogeneity, the model is estimated using an instrumental variable approach, in which the instrument for tutoring is a dummy variable that takes 1 if the student is a first-born child in the family and 0 otherwise, regardless of the sex.

There are concerns that birth order fails to be fully exogenous. Studies report birth order effects on academic capability such as IQ, though their presence remains controversial. Furthermore, given that parents favor a certain-parity child (e.g., first-born) over others with respect to observable education investments, it is possible that they may favor the same child along unobservable dimensions, too; for example, while spending more money on tutoring for the first-born, parents may provide better emotional and nonfinancial supports for the first-born than for other siblings. If this is the case, our IV estimates will be biased. Nevertheless, we expect that such a bias is more likely to be upward than downward.

There are three reasons for this expectation. First, if parents favor, say, the first-born with respect to monetary education investments, they will tend to support the same child more over unobservable dimensions as well; thus a correlation between the first-born indicator and the error term of the main equation is more likely to be positive than negative. Second, studies reporting significant birth order effects on intelligence usually show negative rather than positive effects of birth order: older siblings have higher intelligence than younger siblings. Thus there will be a positive, if any, correlation between the first-born indicator and the error term of the main equation. Third, according to table 10.1, the average education and family income of parents are higher among first-borns than among later-born students. Although our regressions control for parents' education and income, they may not fully capture a potential association between birth order and the error term. To the extent that parents of higher education and income tend to affect positively a child's performance, we also expect the correlation between the first-born indicator and the error term to be positive rather than negative. Therefore, given that first-borns are favored in private tutoring expenditures, as empirically found later, using the first-born indicator as an IV is more likely to overstate the effect of private tutoring expenditures than understate it. Our IV estimates can be viewed as the upper limit of the effect of private tutoring.

Estimation Results

Reduced-Form Results by OLS

Basic OLS results of the effect of private tutoring expenditures on student performance are presented in columns 1 and 2 of table 10.2. The associations between tutoring expenditures and percentile test scores (averaged over the three main subjects) are positive but quite small, although significantly different from zero. A 10 percent greater monthly expenditure on private tutoring is related to no more than a 0.1 percentile point higher test score. As explained previously, such an association that is estimated by OLS may not be consistent and causal. Depending on the correlation between tutoring and the error term, the estimate may be biased upward or downward.

As shown in column 2, being a first-born child is not strongly related with higher test scores, even if there is a positive connection. Although examining the significance of the effect of being first-born in an OLS framework is not a formal test for the validity of birth order as an IV—the consistency of the estimated effect of being first-born depends crucially on exogeneity of private tutoring expenditures—this finding is suggestive of the possibility that birth order can be exogenous to the error term.

Table 10.2   OLS and 2SLS Estimates of Effect of Tutoring Expenditures on Performance (birth order as IV)

| Dependent variables: | Reduced form models (OLS) | | | Structural model (2SLS) |
| | Average test score | | Tutoring expenditure (log) | Average test score |
	(1)	(2)	(3)	(4)
Tutoring expenditure	0.097 (0.036)**	0.093 (0.037)*		0.564 (0.393)
First-born child		1.390 (1.101)	2.952 (0.821)**	
Hours of self-study	0.354 (0.049)**	0.353 (0.049)**	0.018 (0.036)	0.345 (0.051)**
Prior quality (Q2)	13.723 (1.575)**	13.565 (1.583)**	3.042 (1.304)*	12.133 (2.275)**
Prior quality (Q3)	21.764 (1.582)**	21.617 (1.586)**	1.526 (1.284)	20.898 (1.953)**
Prior quality (Q4)	34.124 (1.673)**	34.036 (1.677)**	1.269 (1.321)	33.438 (1.953)**
Prior quality missing	19.289 (1.605)**	19.169 (1.608)**	−2.717 (1.260)*	20.449 (2.030)**
Single father	−5.707 (2.383)*	−5.894 (2.380)*	−1.613 (2.251)	−5.135 (3.216)
Single mother	2.181 (2.334)	2.278 (2.338)	−3.019 (1.728)	3.699 (2.756)
Books at home	0.004 (0.002)	0.004 (0.002)	0.001 (0.002)	0.004 (0.003)
Family income	0.002 (0.003)	0.002 (0.003)	0.021 (0.002)**	−0.008 (0.009)
Parents' avg edu	1.067 (0.236)**	1.051 (0.237)**	0.871 (0.169)**	0.640 (0.431)
Parents' avg age	0.061 (0.152)	0.146 (0.166)	0.125 (0.126)	0.087 (0.165)
Age	−2.601 (0.912)**	−2.647 (0.916)**	0.402 (0.683)	−2.837 (0.986)**
Male	0.166 (1.503)	0.266 (1.504)	−0.698 (1.089)	0.595 (1.579)
Only child	−2.624 (2.181)	−3.214 (2.221)	−1.200 (1.635)	−2.648 (2.258)
Number of siblings	−0.068 (0.920)	0.046 (0.929)	−1.647 (0.676)*	0.822 (1.211)
Intercept	39.69 (17.44)*	36.18 (17.52)*	15.72 (13.19)	28.78 (20.58)
School characteristics	Yes	Yes	Yes	Yes
F (IVs excluded from the 2nd stage)			12.92	
R-square	0.377	0.378	0.244	0.301
Number of samples	1,480	1,480	1,480	1,480

Source: Author's calculations.
Note: Standard errors are reported in parentheses.
* indicates that the estimate is significant at the 0.05 level
** indicates that the estimate is significant at the 0.01 level.

First-Stage Results

The results of the first-stage regression of tutoring expenditures are presented in column 3 of table 10.2. Being first-born significantly and positively affects private tutoring expenditures for a student. First-born students receive about 30 percent greater expenditures on tutoring than later-born students. (Recall that a log of a monthly tutoring expenditure is multiplied by 10.) Provided that being first-born has no direct association with test scores, this variable can serve as a legitimate instrument for spending on tutoring.

Other variables that significantly affect expenditures on private tutoring include the number of siblings and the variables reflecting a family's economic strength such as family income and parents' average education level. The negative relationship between sibship size and tutoring expenditures is consistent with a quality/quantity trade-off in fertility (Becker and Lewis 1973). In contrast, hours of self-study, single-parenthood, the number of books at home, parents' age and a student's age, sex, and only-child status do not have a strong association with the amount of tutoring expenditures.

Second-Stage Results

The IV estimate of the effect of tutoring expenditures is shown in column 4 of table 10.2. A 10 percent increase in expenditure enhances a student's performance by 0.54–0.56 percentile points. Evaluated at the mean percentile score (49), they imply a 1.1 percent increase in test score due to a 10 percent increase in expenditure on private tutoring. There is only a modest causal effect of private tutoring expenditures on a student's academic performance.

Although they are statistically indistinguishable from zero, our IV estimate is more than five times greater than the OLS estimates. This implies that the OLS estimates are severely biased downward. Such a bias arises probably because parents tend to spend more for low-performing siblings than for high-performing siblings in a family.

Given such a small effect of private tutoring expenditures, it would be instructive to compare our IV estimates with corresponding estimates of previous studies, precision of the estimates set apart, to gain some perspective on our results. Unfortunately, the existing literature on the effect of private education expenditures on test scores is quite scarce. Thus, we rely on estimates of the effect of *public* school expenditures on student outcomes for comparison.

In the analysis of a randomization experiment on class size (Project STAR), Krueger (1999, table VII) finds that a one student decrease in class size in grades K to 3 leads to a 0.67–0.88 percentile point increase in test score. Evaluated at the mean values of 21 students per class and 51 percentile test score (appendix table), these estimates imply a 2.8 percent to 3.6 percent improvement in test score percentiles due to a 10 percent decrease in class size and the accompanying 10 percent increase in per-pupil expenditure.[7]

In regard to earnings in the labor market, Card and Krueger (1996, p.37) find that a 10 percent increase in public school spending leads to about a 1 percent to 2 percent increase in subsequent earnings. For example, they report that the reduced-form analysis by Card and Krueger (1992) finds a 1.1 percent increase in weekly earnings associated with a 10 percent reduction in the average pupil-teacher ratio.[8] Other researchers find slightly weaker effects on earnings. Betts (1995) suggests that a 10 percent reduction in the average teacher-pupil ratio leads to a 0.4 percent increase in earnings. Grogger (1996) shows that a 10 percent increase in mean spending per student leads to a 0.7 percent increase in wages. Our estimated effect of private tutoring expenditures is fairly comparable with the estimated effects of public school expenditures on earnings, although ours is on the slightly higher side.

Conclusion

To shed light on the effectiveness of education investments on student outcomes, this chapter examines the effect of private tutoring expenditures on student standardized test scores in the Republic of Korea. Given that education expenditures on a student are not exogenously and randomly determined, the chapter exploits the fact that parents favor a certain-parity child (e.g., first-born) in education investments, while the child's academic capability can be little affected by family birth order.

The causal estimates based on IV methods imply that a 10 percent increase in expenditure on private tutoring leads to a 0.56 percentile point improvement in test scores, even though we cannot reject the hypothesis that it is statistically different from zero. Evaluated at the mean value, this amount of effect is equivalent to a 1.1 percent increase in test score percentiles. Even though a correlation may exist between a student's birth order and performance along the dimensions that are not controlled for by observable characteristics, the estimated effect is more likely to be the upper limit of the true effect than the lower limit. Nevertheless, our estimated effect is fairly comparable with the effects of public school expenditures on earnings estimated by previous studies.

Although we find modest effects of private tutoring on academic performance in Korea, such results are not of course definitive concerning potential impacts of education investments on outcomes. Whether monetary education investments raise student performance in different contexts remains to be further examined.

Notes

1. Kang (2007, section 2) offers more extensive discussions about the possibility of birth order being employed as an IV for educational investments and potential biases that can arise.

2. We cannot reject the hypothesis that this coefficient is statistically different from zero.

3. For an overview of secondary education and private tutoring in South Korea, see Kim and Lee (2001) and OECD (1998).

4. For 2004, general high school accounts for 70.5 percent of 1.75 million high school students in the nation; vocational high school accounts for the rest (*Yearbook of Educational Statistics 2004*, National Statistical Office).

5. These students are also likely to be poor performers in such a general subject test as the CSAT.

6. The KEEP survey asks the monthly average amount of overall expenditures on private tutoring during the last 6 months before grade 12—roughly 9 to 14 months before the CSAT test.

7. Krueger (2003, F55-F56) infers that a 1 percent decrease in class size will be converted into an approximately 1 percent increase in annual per-pupil cost. Compared with Krueger's (1999) estimates, our estimated effect of private tutoring expenditures is no more than half.

8. Our estimated effect of tutoring expenditures is dwarfed by a meta-analysis by Hedges et al. (1994) that yields an estimate that a 10 percent increase in public school expenditure produces an improvement in student performance of approximately 0.7 standard deviations. This amount is equivalent to a 15.9 percentile point improvement in test score in our metric. The summary in Hedges et al. (1994) is, however, criticized by Hanushek (1997) for being biased in favor of large positive effects of school expenditures.

References

Altonji, J. G., T. E. Elder, C. R. Taber. 2005. "An Evaluation of Instrumental Variable Strategies for Estimating the Effects of Catholic Schooling." *Journal of Human Resources* 40 (4): 791–821.

Baker, D. P., M. Akiba, G. K. LeTendre, A. W. Wiseman. 2001. "Worldwide Shadow Education: Outside-School Learning, Institutional Quality of Schooling, and Cross-National Mathematics Achievement." *Educational Evaluation and Policy Analysis* 23 (1): 1–17.

Becker, G. S., and H. G. Lewis. 1973. "On the Interaction between the Quantity and Quality of Children." *Journal of Political Economy* 81 (2, Pt 2): S279–S288.

Betts, J. R. 1995. "Does School Quality Matter? Evidence from the National Longitudinal Survey of Youth." *Review of Economics and Statistics* 77 (2): 231–50.

———. 1996. Is There a Link between School Inputs and Earnings? Fresh Scrutiny of an Old Literature." In *Does Money Matter? The Effect of School Resources on Student Achievement and Adult Success*, ed. G. Burtless, 141–91. Washington, DC: Brookings.

Bray, M. 1999. "The Shadow Education System: Private Tutoring and Its Implications for Planners." UNESCO International Institute for Educational Planning, Paris.

Card, D., and A. B. Krueger. 1992. "Does School Quality Matter? Returns to Education and the Characteristics of Public Schools in the United States." *Journal of Political Economy* 100 (1): 1–40.

———. 1996. "School Resources and Student Outcomes: An Overview of the Literature and New Evidence from North and South Carolina." *Journal of Economic Perspectives* 10 (4): 31–50.

Grogger, J. 1996. "School Expenditures and Post-Schooling Earnings: Evidence from High School and Beyond." *Review of Economics and Statistics* 78 (4): 628–37.

Hanushek, E. A. 1997. "Assessing the Effects of School Resources on Student Performance: An Update." *Educational Evaluation and Policy Analysis* 19 (2): 141–64.

———. 2003. "The Failure of Input-Based Schooling Policies." *Economic Journal* 113 (485): F64–F98.

Hedges, L. V., R. D. Laine, and R. Greenwald. 1994. "Does Money Matter? A Meta-analysis of Studies of the Effects of Differential School Inputs on Student Outcomes." *Educational Researcher* 23 (3): 5–14.

Kang, C. 2007. "Does Money Matter? The Effect of Private Educational Expenditures on Academic Performance." Working paper. Department of Economics, National University of Singapore.

KEDI (Korean Educational Development Institute). 1998. *Survey on Educational Expenditures*. Seoul, Republic of Korea (in Korean).

Kim, S., and J.-H. Lee. 2001. "Demand for Education and Developmental State: Private Tutoring in South Korea." Social Science Research Network Electronic Paper Collection. http://ssrn.com/abstract=268284.

Krueger, A. B. 1999. "Experimental Estimates of Education Production Functions." *Quarterly Journal of Economics* 114 (2): 497–532.

———. 2003. "Economic Considerations and Class Size." *Economic Journal* 113 (485): F34-F62.

Ministry of Education. 2000. *Sakyoyuk Siltae Josa* [*Survey on Private Tutoring in 1999*]. Seoul, Republic of Korea (in Korean).

OECD (Organisation for Economic Co-operation and Development). 1998. "Reviews of National Policies for Education: Korea." OECD Publications, Paris.

Time Asia. 2006. "Asia's Overscheduled Kids." 167 (12): 48–55.

CHAPTER 11

Comparing the Private Cost of Education at Public, Private, and Faith-Based Schools in Cameroon

Prospere Backiny-Yetna and Quentin Wodon

Introduction

It is often argued that faith-based organizations (FBOs) provide a substantial share of education, health, and other social services in African countries, that they do so at a lower cost than the public sector, that the services provided by FBOs are of better quality than those of the public sector, and finally that these services tend to be better targeted toward the poor than is the case for the public sector (and certainly for the private sector). If all of those assertions are correct, they have clear implications for policy, as donors as well as governments should then be more inclined than is currently the case to support FBOs in their service delivery activities.

As discussed in part 2 of this book, there is some evidence that faith-based and more generally private schools achieve a better outcome for their students than public schools and contribute to a more competitive marketplace for education services (e.g., Altonji et al. 2005; Cox and Jimenez 1990; Evans and Schwab 1995; González and Arévalo 2005; Hsieh and Urquiola 2006; and Hoxby 1994).

Yet in this book, the evidence provided on faith-based schools is mixed. Allcott and Ortega (2009) suggest that in R. B. de Venezuela, Fe y Alegría schools perform slightly better on standardized test scores than public schools, but the difference between the two sets of schools is limited, and although Fe y Alegría schools are in principle targeting poor neighborhoods, the data suggest few differences in the characteristics of the students served by both sets of schools. In Bangladesh, Asadullah et al. (2009) suggest that there are few differences in test scores between religious (madrasas) and secular schools when selection into religious school is taken into account, but they document a statistically significant learning deficit for graduates of primary madrasas, who tend to have lower test scores in secondary schools even after controlling for school- and classroom-specific unobservable correlates of learning. Wodon and Ying (2009) show that in Sierra Leone, faith-based schools do reach the poor much better than public schools, and that after appropriate controls to take into account the characteristics of students and endogenous school choice, faith-based schools also perform marginally better than public schools in promoting literacy and numeracy among students. By contrast Backiny-Yetna and Wodon (2009) suggest that in the Democratic Republic of Congo, there are no systematic differences between faith-based and public schools in serving poor as opposed to nonpoor students, with also small differences in quality that tend not to be statistically significant.

Apart from the issue of the comparative performance of students from different schools, there has also been some work in the literature on the cost of services for their users, and how this cost, or the level of the service provided, varies between faith-based and public providers. In their analysis of health service provision in Uganda, Reinikka and Svensson (forthcoming) use a change in financing of not-for-profit health care providers through untied grants to test two theories of organizational behavior. The first theory postulates that not-for-profit providers are intrinsically motivated to serve the poor and will therefore use new resources to expand their services or cut the cost of these services. The second theory postulates that not-for-profit providers are captured by their managers or workers and behave like for-profit actors. Although they may not appropriate profits, they would tend to use untied grants to raise the salaries of their staff or provide them with other benefits that would not directly serve the poor. The authors' empirical results suggest that the first altruistic theory is validated by the data, and that the results matter in the sense that this altruistic difference makes a difference for the poor.

In this chapter, using recent household survey data for Cameroon, we focus on measuring the cost for households of the education services that their children receive and assessing how this cost varies according to the type of service provider. Thus, although we provide basic statistics on the performance of various types of schools, we focus our econometric analysis on the estimation of the private cost of education. We do so because contrary to what is observed in some other countries, the data suggest that faith-based schools in Cameroon serve primarily better-off children, with public schools serving the poor better (private schools are even more tilted toward better-off students, but that is to be expected). Cameroon is a country in which the state provides subsidies to faith-based schools, but not to private schools. However, subsidies provided per student to faith-based schools in Cameroon are typically smaller than the subsidies provided to public schools. This means that faith-based schools have to raise more funds than public schools to be sustainable, which makes them more expensive for parents than public schools and results in a weaker targeting performance in reaching the poor (for details on education in Cameroon, see among others World Bank 2003, 2005).

How much more expensive are faith-based schools in comparison with public schools? To answer that question, basic statistics are not enough because we need to use proper econometric techniques to control for the endogeneity of school choice. What is meant by endogeneity is the fact that the choice of school by parents depends itself on the cost of the schools. Because faith-based schools are more expensive than public schools, parents who can afford these schools are likely to be able and willing to spend more on the education of their children, all other things being equal. This will typically generate an upward bias in the estimation of the cost of faith-based schools for parents if no controls for endogeneity are used in the econometric analysis. Our econometric methodology enables us to avoid such bias and obtain more reasonable comparisons of costs than would be obtained without such an approach.

This chapter is structured as follows. In the next section, we provide basic statistics on the key variables of interest for the analysis, including the market share of the various types of schools, the satisfaction rates of parents with the schools, and the costs of attending the schools. The subsequent section provides the results of our econometric analysis to assess the cost differential between different schools after controlling for the characteristics of the children and their households, as well as the endogenous choice of the school attended by the children. A brief conclusion follows.

Basic Statistics

We focus our analysis on primary schools. The data are from the nationally representative ECAM 3 survey implemented by the Institut National de la Statistique in 2007. Tables 11.1 and 11.2 provide data on the market shares of various types of school providers by quintile of per capita consumption (with the first quintile, "Q1," representing the poorest 20 percent of the population, and the top quintile, "Q5," the richest 20 percent) and by the religious affiliation of the children. Given that the proportion of the population in poverty is at 39.9 percent according to official estimates from the National Statistical Office, the first two quintiles can be considered as representing the poor.

Faith-based providers account for 14 percent of all primary school students in urban areas and 11 percent in rural areas (12 percent at the national level). The market share of public government schools is 86 percent in rural areas (in which private schools are virtually nonexistent) and 57 percent in urban areas (in which private schools account for 29 percent of all students). Thus, although faith-based schools in Cameroon do not have as large a market share as faith-based networks in the Democratic Republic of Congo (Backiny-Yetna and Wodon 2009) or Sierra Leone (Wodon and Ying 2009), their role as service providers is far from negligible.

Table 11.1   Distribution of Students in Primary School by Quintile of per Capita Consumption

	Q1	Q2	Q3	Q4	Q5	All
Urban						
Public	8.4	14.8	26.1	28.6	22.2	100.0
Private	0.5	5.7	15.9	29.3	48.5	100.0
Religious	6.2	10.9	22.7	28.1	32.1	100.0
All	5.8	11.6	22.7	28.7	31.2	100.0
Rural						
Public	34.3	28.9	20.9	12.1	3.7	100.0
Private	20.2	24.4	24.5	24.2	6.7	100.0
Religious	16.1	33.0	24.2	19.2	7.5	100.0
All	31.9	29.2	21.4	13.3	4.2	100.0
Cameroon						
Public	28.1	25.6	22.1	16.1	8.1	100.0
Private	4.3	9.3	17.5	28.3	40.5	100.0
Religious	12.3	24.5	23.6	22.6	17.0	100.0
All	23.5	23.6	21.8	18.2	12.9	100.0

Source: Authors' calculations using ECAM 3 survey for 2007 (INS, Cameroon).

Table 11.2   Distribution of Students by Religion of Their Parents

	Catholic	Protestant	Other Christian	Muslim	Others	All
Urban						
Public	47.9	56.3	50.5	82.3	50.8	57.1
Private	36.9	26.9	34.2	7.2	41.6	28.7
Religious	15.2	16.7	15.3	10.5	7.6	14.3
All	100.0	100.0	100.0	100.0	100.0	100.0
Rural						
Public	80.5	87.8	81.2	90.8	94.4	86.1
Private	3.0	3.6	3.6	4.4	0.7	3.2
Religious	16.6	8.6	15.2	4.7	4.9	10.7
All	100.0	100.0	100.0	100.0	100.0	100.0
Cameroon						
Public	68.1	79.1	72.8	87.9	86.3	76.8
Private	15.8	10.0	11.9	5.4	8.3	11.4
Religious	16.1	10.9	15.2	6.8	5.4	11.9
All	100.0	100.0	100.0	100.0	100.0	100.0

Source: Authors' calculations using ECAM 3 survey for 2007 (INS, Cameroon).

Faith-based schools tend to serve households that are better off compared with government schools. This is visible especially when comparing statistics for students from the bottom quintile in rural areas, because 16 percent of the students in faith-based schools belong to the poorest quintile in rural areas, versus 34 percent for government schools (the differences for the other quintiles are much smaller). In urban areas, differences are largest in the top quintiles, which account for 32 percent of all students in faith-based schools, versus 22 percent for the public sector. As expected, private schools are even more tilted toward children from the top quintiles.

Faith-based schools also tend to serve Catholic and other Christian children proportionately more than other groups, but Muslim and other children also attend those schools. Thus one can argue than in Cameroon as in other countries in which faith-based schools benefit from public funding, there is probably no discrimination by faith-based schools against students on the basis of their religion because the schools aim to cater to the needs of all students.

Although we will focus in the rest of this chapter on the private cost of schooling, it is still useful to provide basic statistics on the performance of faith-based and government schools. Three main outcome indicators can be obtained from the survey: (1) whether students can read and write in English or French (Cameroon is a bilingual country, and the education system supports education in both English and French, with the majority of the students enrolled in French schools); (2) whether students have repeated a grade in the previous year; and (3) whether children are still enrolled at age 15. Table 11.3 provides summary statistics on these three performance indicators. Most parents declare that their children can read or write in either English or French, but the performance of faith-based schools seems to be lower than that of other schools in urban areas and higher in rural areas. In regard to repetition rates, public schools have the lowest at the national and urban levels, and in rural areas the repetition rate seems higher among faith-based schools. Faith-based schools have the highest drop-out rates in all areas, with more than 20 percent of students dropping out in the rural areas.

Table 11.4 provides data on the private costs of schooling by education provider. The data for Cameroon are especially rich in this respect, as it is feasible to identify the cost of schooling for each child, as opposed to only having data for the household as a whole. We focus on the expenditures that are directly paid to the schools because that is what is

Table 11.3   Student Performance by Type of School

	% of students		
	Who can read and write in French or English (grade 2 to 6)	Who have not repeated a grade in the previous year (grade 1 to 6)	Who are still enrolled in school at age 15 (all grades)
Urban			
Public	92.5	75.9	94.0
Private	95.3	84.4	94.5
Religious	89.3	78.3	89.3
All	92.8	78.7	93.7
Rural			
Public	79.1	66.3	92.1
Private	73.2	74.5	86.2
Religious	83.7	76.2	78.8
All	79.5	67.6	90.9
Cameroon			
Public	82.5	68.6	92.6
Private	91.2	82.5	92.7
Religious	85.9	77.1	82.8
All	83.9	71.2	91.9

Source: Authors' calculations using ECAM 3 survey for 2007 implemented by the INS, Cameroon.

Table 11.4   Annual Education Expenditure (fees and related) by Student and by Type of School (in Franc CFA)

	Registration	Fees	Parent association	Other	All
Urban					
Public	1,372	939	2,816	708	5,864
Private	7,313	38,141	1,609	1,418	49,420
Religious	4,198	17,152	1,839	1,107	24,818
All	3,504	14,157	2,333	969	21,181
Rural					
Public	496	286	2,402	447	3,674
Private	3,604	13,248	1,163	401	19,400
Religious	1,714	8,454	984	525	11,571
All	730	1,612	2,218	453	5,051
Cameroon					
Public	707	443	2,502	510	4,199
Private	6,576	33,184	1,520	1,215	43,499
Religious	2,703	11,857	1,325	762	16,717
All	1,633	5,689	2,255	621	10,257

Source: Authors' calculation using ECAM 3 survey for 2007 implemented by the INS, Cameroon.

affected by the type of funding that the schools receive from the government (as explained earlier, a key reason for the higher cost of faith-based as opposed to public schools is the fact that, although faith-based schools are subsidized, they do not benefit from subsidies as much as public schools do).

Table 11.4 shows that private schools are by far the most expensive, but faith-based schools are significantly more expensive than public schools in both urban and rural areas. Most of the differences in costs are related to registration fees, and especially other fees. By contrast, fees for parent associations and other costs are not too different between the various types of schools. The various fees paid to schools represent most of the private cost of schooling for households (however, those data are available only for the household as a whole and not by child); other expenses include the cost of uniforms, transport, books and materials, and the like. The proportion of the formal fees paid to schools to the total private costs of schooling, which is at 43 percent for the sample as a whole, is fairly stable across well-being quintiles.

Looking at the data in table 11.4, one could be led to believe that faith-based schools are about four times more expensive than public schools in urban areas and three times more expensive in rural areas. However, such simple cost comparisons between the two types of schools do not account for the fact that there are potentially important differences in the types of students that enroll in public and faith-based schools. As mentioned earlier, students enrolled in government schools tend to be from poorer backgrounds than students in faith-based schools. Parents of poorer students are likely to spend less on schools for obvious reasons. The key question is, whether by controlling for the characteristics of the students and their households and taking into account endogeneity in the choice of school attended by children (this depends on the cost of schools for parents), are faith-based schools still more expensive than government schools? To answer that question, we turn to an econometric analysis in the next section.

Econometric Analysis

Our technique for assessing the correlates of cost is simple. We estimate a linear regression model on the logarithm of the cost of schooling (taking into account only the various fees paid to schools as outlined in table 11.4). Because the choice of school for a child depends on cost, we instrument the choice of the type of school the child goes to through probit regressions, which include as regressors all the correlates of the cost regression plus the leave-out share of the students in the child's geographic area that are going to faith-based or private schools. The child's geographic area is identified through the primary sampling unit to which the household belongs in the survey (typically each primary sampling unit includes between 20 and 30 households). We compute the leave-out participation rate in faith-based schools not taking into account whether the child himself or herself goes (thus, for each child in the same primary sampling unit, we compute a different leave-out participation rate).[1]

The results for the determinants of the type of school attended are not shown but are available on request. The leave-out market shares of different types of schools at the PSU level are key determinants of the type of school the child attends. In addition, students in the Anglophone system are more likely to go to private schools, whereas students in rural areas are less likely to do so. Very young and older children are more likely to go to public schools than to private and faith-based schools. Catholics are more likely to enroll in religious schools, whereas all other groups are less likely to do so. There are strong geographic effects, with the probability of going to private schools highest in Douala, and the probability of going to religious schools higher elsewhere. Children in higher grades are more likely to be enrolled in private or religious schools, as opposed to public schools. More often wealthier households send their children to private and religious schools. The education of the household head is not a key determinant of school choice, except when the head has a university education, in which case the child is more likely to go to a private or religious school. The sector of occupation of the head does not have a statistically significant impact on the type of school the child attends.

We focus here on the results of the cost regressions (see table A11.1 in the annex). The regressors or correlates of the cost are (1) the type of school attended by the child (this variable is instrumented as explained above to avoid endogeneity issues); (2) the grade in school the child is attending (with the first grade of the cycle being the reference category); (3) characteristics of the child—the age of the child and the age squared, the sex of the child, whether the child lives with his or her biological family; (4) the geographic location of the child according to urban or rural status and the main areas in the country (with Douala as the reference category); (5) the quintile of per capita consumption of the household in which the child lives; (6) household demographic variables—whether the household head is male or female; (7) the education level of the household head; and (8) the socioeconomic group of the household head.

The key variable of interest is the impact on cost of the type of school attended by the child. Without instruments, the premium for private and religious schools over public schools is very high, with private schools about three times as expensive as public schools and religious schools at least twice as expensive. With instruments, the differences are much smaller, but still large. Thus instrumenting the regressions reduced as expected the differential in costs. Private schools cost about 47 percent more than public schools, and the premium for religious schools is at 40 percent. Other key drivers of cost include the fact of studying in the Anglophone system (increase in cost of 18 percent) or being located in Douala or Yaoundé (with Yaoundé more expensive than Douala, and Douala more expensive than the other areas). The higher the grade the child is in, the higher the cost is, with an especially large increase in cost in grade 6. Better-off households tend to spend more, as proxied by the quintiles of per capita consumption. When the household head has achieved secondary education or a higher level, the household also spends more for the child's schooling. The occupation of the household head is less of a factor.

Conclusion

The objective of this chapter was to provide a comparative assessment of the cost of faith-based, private, and government schools in Cameroon. Contrary to what has been observed in some other African countries such as Sierra Leone, religious schools in Cameroon are less targeted toward the poor than public schools. This is probably in part because they are more expensive, and in turn the cost of religious schools may be related to the fact that, although they benefit from public subsidies, these subsidies are not as large as for public schools.

Simple basic statistics suggest that in regard to the fees that must be paid to the schools, faith-based schools are about four times more expensive than public schools in urban areas and three times more expensive in rural areas. Private schools are even more expensive. Regression results without controls for the endogeneity of school choice suggest as well very large differences in costs between public and faith-based and private schools. Yet once controls for endogeneity of school choice are introduced, the differences in costs, although still large, are reduced substantially. The results suggest that private schools cost 47 percent more than public schools, and the premium for religious schools is at 40 percent.

Our results could have implications for policy, but before discussing any such implications, for example, in terms of the financing of faith-based schools, substantial additional contextual work would need to be done. These results are also interesting in the African context. It is often argued that faith-based schools serve the poor better than public schools. Although this may be true in some countries, it is not in others such as Cameroon. Detailed country-level work is needed to better document the role of faith-based schools in education systems before making any generalization on the services they provide, be it in regard to their performance or to their cost.

Annex: Regression Results

Table A11.1   Determinants of the Logarithm of Education Expenditure

	Noninstrumented model			Instrumented model		
	Coef.	Std. Err.	P>t	Coef.	Std. Err.	P>t
Private school*	1.8374	0.0239	***	0.4680	0.0227	***
Religious school*	1.3828	0.0198	***	0.4011	0.0167	***
Anglophone system (yes)	0.2362	0.0280	***	0.1864	0.0380	***
Rural (yes)	−0.1339	0.0165	***	−0.0096	0.0238	
Region						
Douala						
Yaoundé	0.2364	0.0376	***	0.1423	0.0530	***
Adamaoua	−0.6369	0.0417	***	−0.7317	0.0682	***
Centre	−0.2120	0.0383	***	−0.4643	0.0589	***
Est	−0.5453	0.0404	***	−0.6616	0.0665	***
Extrême-nord	−0.7448	0.0370	***	−0.7157	0.0645	***
Littoral	−0.2329	0.0421	***	−0.4447	0.0680	***
Nord	−0.6469	0.0398	***	−0.6445	0.0681	***
Nord-ouest	−0.6487	0.0433	***	−0.8648	0.0678	***
Ouest	−0.4922	0.0346	***	−0.7385	0.0551	***
Sud	−0.4568	0.0413	***	−0.5538	0.0680	***
Sud-ouest	−0.3657	0.0440	***	−0.5894	0.0668	***
Grade						
Grade 1						
Grade 2	−0.0534	0.0212	**	−0.0415	0.0283	
Grade 3	−0.0329	0.0216		0.0191	0.0290	
Grade 4	−0.0051	0.0223		0.0317	0.0299	
Grade 5	0.0522	0.0220	**	0.1000	0.0299	***
Grade 6	0.7755	0.0231	***	0.8221	0.0313	***
Quintile						
Q1						
Q2	0.1005	0.0218	***	0.0529	0.0293	*
Q3	0.1269	0.0221	***	0.0142	0.0298	
Q4	0.1803	0.0238	***	0.0053	0.0333	
Q5	0.3776	0.0272	***	0.1904	0.0395	***
Female head hh (yes)	0.0299	0.0157	*	0.0245	0.0208	
Education hh						
No education						
Primary incomplete	0.0571	0.0208	***	0.0497	0.0277	*
Primary complete	0.0158	0.0232		−0.0363	0.0311	

(continued)

Table A11.1   Determinants of the Logarithm of Education Expenditure (Continued)

	Noninstrumented model			Instrumented model		
	Coef.	Std. Err.	P>t	Coef.	Std. Err.	P>t
Secondary 1	0.0603	0.0226	***	0.0089	0.0302	
Secondary 2	0.1230	0.0270	***	0.0751	0.0364	**
University	0.2125	0.0363	***	0.1793	0.0490	***
Socioeconomic group						
Unemployed						
Wage earner, formal	−0.0790	0.0335	**	−0.0460	0.0445	
Independent agriculture	−0.0986	0.0310	***	0.0073	0.0416	
Employer, nonagriculture	−0.0169	0.0502		−0.0236	0.0669	
Own worker, nonagriculture	−0.0495	0.0312		−0.0080	0.0415	
Dependent, informal	−0.0881	0.0379	**	−0.0568	0.0505	
Student	0.0743	0.0670		0.1347	0.0892	
Constant	1.3727	0.0481	**	3.1850	0.0687	***
Statistics						
Number of observations	9542			9524		
R^2	0.7041			0.4765		

Source: Authors' calculation using ECAM 3 survey for 2007 implemented by the INS, Cameroon.

Note

1. As noted in earlier chapters of this book, this strategy of identifying the outcome regression through a leave-out mean PSU-level variable affecting the choice of an individual was used, among others, by Ravallion and Wodon (2000) in their work on schooling and child labor in Bangladesh and by Wodon (2000) in work on the impact of low income energy policies on the probability of electricity disconnection in France.

References

Allcott, H., and D. E. Ortega. 2009. "The Performance of Decentralized School Systems: Evidence from Fe y Alegría in Venezuela." In *Emerging Evidence on Private Participation in Education: Vouchers and Faith-Based Providers*, ed. F. Barrera-Osorio, H. A. Patrinos, and Q. Wodon. Washington, DC: World Bank.

Altonji, J. G., T. E. Elder, and C. R. Taber. 2005. "An Evaluation of Instrumental Variable Strategies for Estimating the Effects of Catholic Schooling." *Journal of Human Resources* 40 (4): 791–821.

Asadullah, M. N., N. Chaudhury, and A. Dar. 2009. "Student Achievement in Religious and Secular Secondary Schools in Bangladesh." In *Emerging Evidence on Private Participation in Education: Vouchers and Faith-Based Providers*, ed. F. Barrera-Osorio, H. A. Patrinos, and Q. Wodon. Washington, DC: World Bank.

Backiny-Yetna, P., and Q. Wodon. 2009. "Comparing Faith-Based and Government Schools in the Democratic Republic of Congo." In *Emerging Evidence on Private Participation in Education: Vouchers and Faith-Based Providers*, ed. F. Barrera-Osorio, H. A. Patrinos, and Q. Wodon. Washington, DC: World Bank.

Cox, D., and E. Jimenez. 1990. "The Relative Effectiveness of Private and Public Schools: Evidence from Two Developing Countries." *Journal of Development Economics* 34 (1–2) (November): 99–121.

Evans, W., and R. Schwab. 1995. "Finishing High School and Starting College: Do Catholic Schools Make a Difference?" *Quarterly Journal of Economics* 110 (4) (November): 941–74.

González, R. A., and G. Arévalo. 2005. "Subsidized Catholic Schools in Venezuela." In *Private Education and Public Policy in Latin America*, ed. L. Wolff, J. C. Navarro, and P. González. Washington, DC: Project for Educational Revitalization in the Americas.

Hoxby, C. M. 1994. "Do Private Schools Provide Competition for Public Schools?" NBER (National Bureau of Economic Research) Working Paper 4978. NBER, Cambridge, MA.

Hsieh, C., and M. Urquiola. 2006. "The Effects of Generalized School Choice on Achievement and Stratification: Evidence from Chile's School Voucher Program." *Journal of Public Economics* 90: 1477–1503.

Ravallion M., and Q. Wodon. 2000. "Does Child Labor Displace Schooling? Evidence on Behavioral Responses to an Enrollment Subsidy." *Economic Journal* 110: C158–75.

Reinikka, R., and J. Svensson. 2009. "Working for God? Evidence from a Change in Financing of Not-for-Profit Health Care Providers in Uganda." *Journal of the European Economic Association*, forthcoming.

Wodon Q. 2000. "Low Income Energy Assistance and Disconnection in France." *Applied Economics Letters* 7: 775–79.

Wodon, Q., and Y. Ying. 2009. "Literacy and Numeracy in Faith-Based and Government Schools in Sierra Leone." In *Emerging Evidence on Private*

Participation in Education: Vouchers and Faith-Based Providers, ed. F. Barrera-Osorio, H. A. Patrinos, and Q. Wodon. Washington, DC: World Bank.

World Bank. 2003. Rapport d'Etat du Système Educatif Camerounais: Eléments de diagnostic pour la politique éducative dans le contexte de l'EPT et du DSRP. Mimeo. World Bank, Washington, DC.

———. 2005. *République du Cameroun: Acquis et défis dans la lutte contre la pauvreté*. Report No. 32820-CM.

Index